HUNTINGDONSHIRE PUBS

THROUGH TIME

Alan Akeroyd &
Caroline Clifford

AMBERLEY PUBLISHING

Acknowledgements

Most of the old photographs in this book have come from the collections held at Huntingdon Library and Archives, where they are freely available for consultation alongside many thousands of other historical documents, maps and published resources. Huntingdon Library and Archives is a Cambridgeshire Libraries Service, provided by Cambridgeshire County Council. If you would like to see or purchase a copy of any of the originals, please visit the Archives.

Some photographs have come from other sources. We would like to thank Bob Burn-Murdoch, Curator of the Norris Museum in St Ives; David and Alexa Cox of Huntingdon; the Shakespeare at the George Trust; and the Huntingdon Community Archive. We are also grateful to Soo Martin of the FSB Scanning Bureau, to Ken and Pam Sneath for giving us a sneak preview of *Thirsty Godmanchester*, and all our colleagues at Huntingdonshire Archives.

First published 2012

Amberley Publishing
The Hill, Stroud
Gloucestershire, GL5 4EP

www.amberley-books.com

Copyright © Alan Akeroyd & Caroline Clifford, 2012

The right of Alan Akeroyd & Caroline Clifford to be identified as the Authors of this work has been asserted in accordance with the Copyrights, Designs and Patents Act 1988.

ISBN 978 1 4456 0560 9

British Library Cataloguing in Publication Data.
A catalogue record for this book is available from the British Library.

Typeset in 9.5pt on 12pt Celeste.
Typesetting by Amberley Publishing.
Printed in the UK.

Introduction

Huntingdonshire's economy has largely depended on the major roads and waterways which run through the county, so it is no surprise that the oldest and largest surviving drinking places are travellers' inns. Two major roads linking London with the north crossed the Great Ouse in Huntingdonshire, namely the Great North Road (the predecessor of what is now the A1) and the Old North Road, which largely followed the route of the Roman Ermine Street. Both roads carried a large amount of stagecoach traffic during the height of the turnpike road system, with long distance mail and stagecoaches stopping overnight in the great coaching inns, such as the 'Lion' and the 'George' at Buckden, or the 'Bridge' and the 'George' at Huntingdon. Charles I made the 'George' at Huntingdon his army's HQ in August 1645 and it is reputed that Dick Turpin stayed there at times.

Historically, inns concentrated more on the needs of travellers and their horses, while public houses tended to focus more on the social drinking needs of the local population. The distinction was never hard and fast, however, and many pubs could offer a basic level of accommodation. The social divisions of the local community were often reflected in the interior arrangement of a pub, so that labourers would drink in the minimally-furnished public bar or tap room, while the more well-to-do would sit on proper cushioned chairs in the saloon, and pay a penny or two more for their drinks. Some pubs had a snug area, where women could drink in private or couples could meet away from prying eyes.

The main reason for the popularity of alcohol was the lack of a reliable and clean water supply. Beer was much safer to drink than water, and was so weak that even some temperance movements accepted it. The problems to society came not from beer but from gin, which became cheap enough in the late eighteenth and early nineteenth centuries for people to drink instead of either beer or water, and which contributed towards much public drunkenness. The Beerhouse Act was therefore passed in 1830, encouraging householders to brew and sell their own beer in an attempt to cut back on gin. The new beerhouses catered for the agricultural and industrial poor of the Victorian era.

Traditional English pub names, such as 'The Royal Oak', were eschewed by the beerhouses in favour of more imaginative or evocative names such as 'Speed The Plough'. The most popular name, however, was that of the sovereign who signed the Beerhouse Act: 'King William IV'. Many of the pubs illustrated in this book began life as simple beerhouses.

By the 1860s so many beerhouses had been created that the law was changed to make it harder to set one up. The core requirement of all the UK's current licensing laws – that in order to run a public house you need first to obtain a licence from a magistrate – was introduced in 1869 and has remained in force ever since. During the twentieth century the beerhouses gradually died away, either shutting their doors or successfully applying for a full licence as a proper pub. This development happened in parallel with the improvements in the cleanliness of Britain's drinking water, so that the health benefits of weak beer became less important. The final provisions of the 1830 Beerhouse Act were repealed in 1993.

Many of the old photographs in this book were taken by Huntingdon Brewery Ltd during the early 1930s as a photographic record of their tied houses. The series of photographs taken by the brewery is a unique historical resource as it includes shots of both the front and back of many pubs.

The number of pubs has greatly declined since the Victorian heyday. In the late nineteenth century Huntingdon had nearly thirty pubs or beerhouses for a population of just over 4,000 people. Today Huntingdon has a population five times the size, but only eleven pubs. Most of this decline happened in the second half of the twentieth century. The 1940 edition of *Kelly's Directory* lists no fewer than 300 public houses in Huntingdonshire, serving an overall population of nearly 60,000 people. Today there are barely 100 pubs, serving a population of over 167,000. The most famous recent closure has been the 'Falcon' in Huntingdon, a sixteenth-century inn that closed its doors in December 2008.

Over time many of Huntingdonshire's inns, pubs and beerhouses have been demolished or put to other uses. In these pages you will see pubs that have become private houses, such as the 'Oddfellows Arms' in Sawtry; pubs that have become shops, such as the 'Royal Oak' in St Neots; pubs that have become the bases for other businesses, such as the 'Whistling Pig' near Warboys; and pubs which have simply been demolished, such as the 'Three Tuns' in St Ives, of which just a fragment of one wall remains. But, scattered here and there, are pubs which have successfully remained pubs. Cheers!

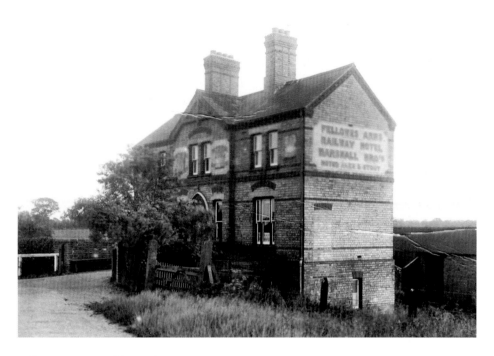

Fellowes Arms – Abbots Ripton

The Fellowes family acquired the former Ramsey Abbey estate in 1737. They left Ramsey and made Abbots Ripton Hall their main home in 1931 and have lived there ever since. The 'Fellowes Arms' stood next to the railway station. It was near here that the Abbots Ripton rail disaster took place in 1876, when heavy snow led to a failure of the signals and the *Flying Scotsman* ploughed in to a coal train. A Leeds train then crashed into the wreckage. Thirteen people were killed and twenty-four injured. The isolated hostelry is now a private house.

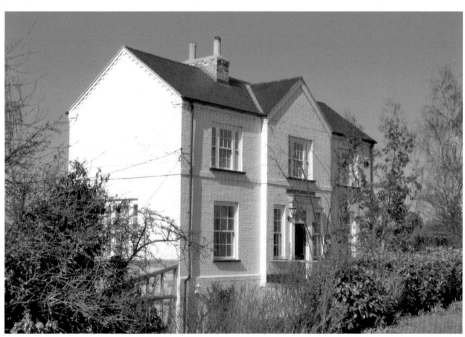

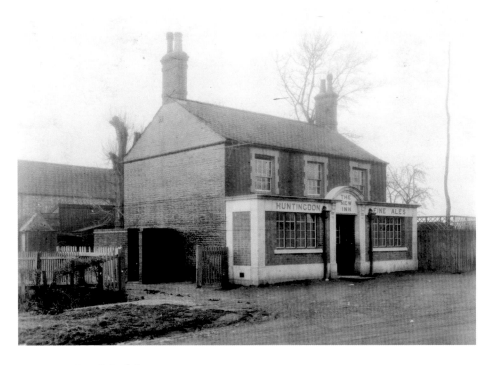

New Inn – Brook End, Brampton

'The New Inn' was originally built as a cottage in 1824, but by 1895 it had become an alehouse. It later became known as 'The Harrier'. In September 2004, it was purchased by Dinesh and Mukesh Makwana, who had lived in Huntingdon since the 1970s. The pub was fully refurbished and opened as the 'Masala Bar and Restaurant' in January 2005.

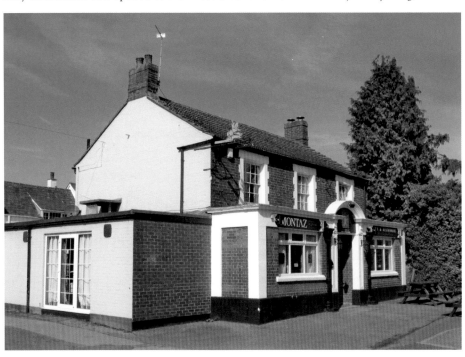

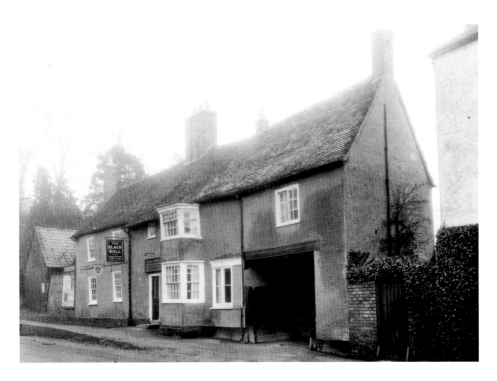

The Black Bull – Church Road, Brampton

'The Black Bull' is a former coaching inn dating from the sixteenth century. Samuel Pepys, who lived nearby, described the inn's beer as 'fresh with a taste of worme wood which ever did please me very well'. Pubs in Brampton were well patronised. The Chairman of the Huntingdonshire Assessment Committee commented in 1933 that 'the village seemed to be the aristocratic part of the county on account of the amount of spirits consumed'. 'The Black Bull' is still a pub.

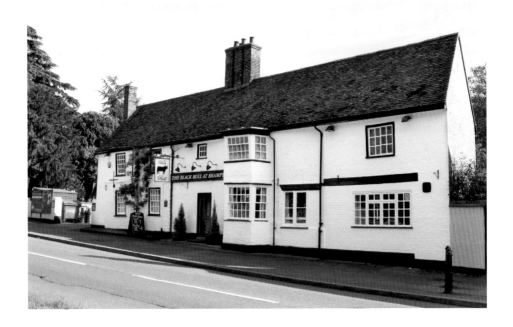

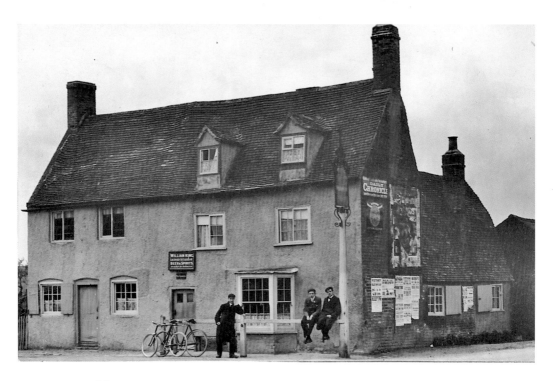

Brampton Hut (1)

There has been an inn on this site for centuries, at the cross roads of the Great North Road and the east-west route from East Anglia to the Midlands. It was originally known as 'Creamer's Hut', but by 1851 it was called 'Brampton Hut'. The later photograph, taken in 1984, shows the motel which was built adjacent to the old 'Brampton Hut Inn'.

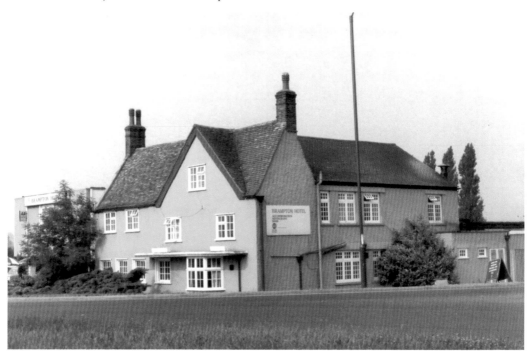

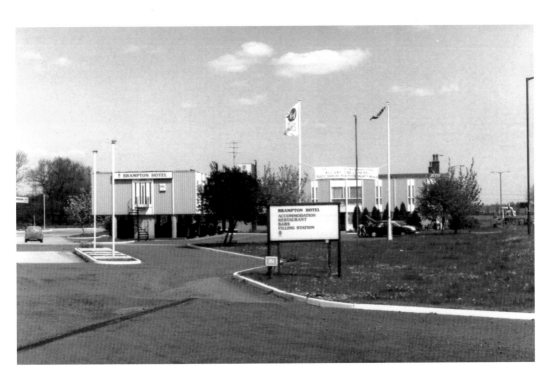

Brampton Hut (2)

The motel closed in the 1990s and was demolished during the widening of the A1, but the name lives on. The new 'Brampton Hut interchange' was created following the opening of the A1/M1 link road in 1994 and now features a Premier Inn, Table Table restaurant, McDonald's and a service station.

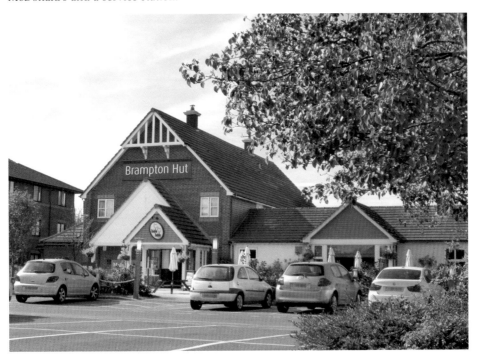

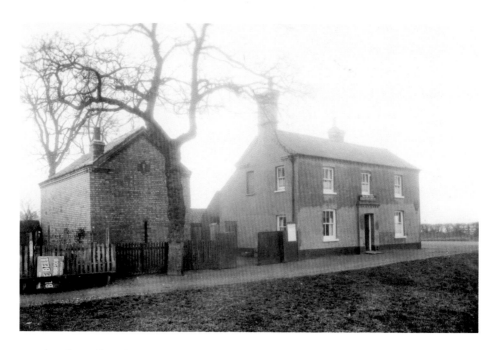

Royal Oak – Bell End, Brampton

'The Royal Oak' had previously been known as the 'King Charles'. There was a large oak tree with a seat under it next to the pub – perhaps this is why it changed its name. The tree stood next to a green where the brass band would practice. The green was replaced by the roundabout in the 1930s and the 'Royal Oak' itself was replaced by houses on the Glebe estate when it closed in the 1970s. It is one of at least nine pubs in Brampton which have disappeared. The new photograph is of modern housing in Budge Close, on the site of the former 'Royal Oak'.

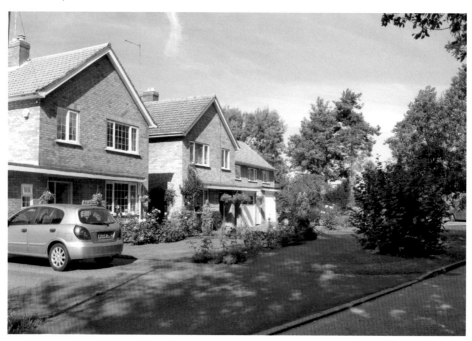

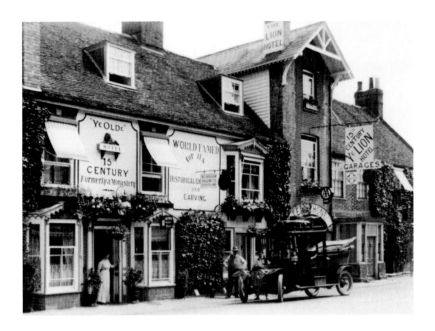

Lion Hotel – Buckden

'The Lion' may have been built as a guest house for the Bishop of Lincoln. Nearby Buckden Towers was a palace belonging to the Bishops, a convenient stopping place on the way to London. In the early days of motoring the inn took full advantage of its history, claiming to be a former monastery (which it was not) and 'world famed for its historical oak ceiling and carving'. Some ancient carvings on the ceiling beams still survive. At times it has also been called the 'Lion and Lamb' and the 'Lamb and Flag.' It is still a hotel today.

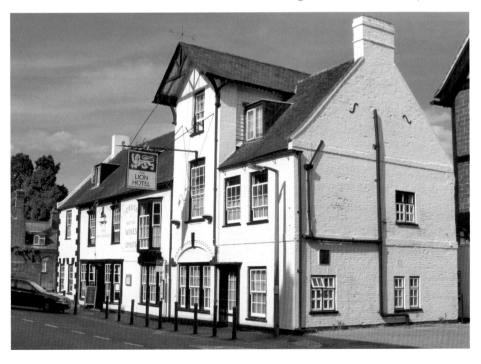

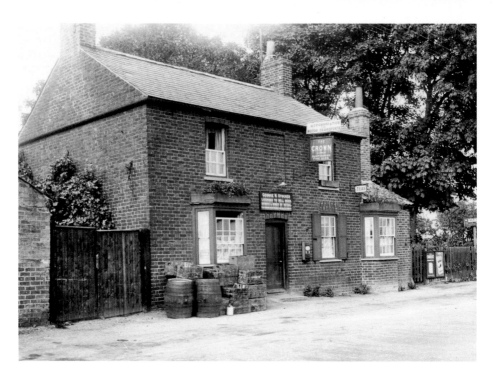

The Crown – Great North Road, Buckden

Otherwise known as the 'Crown Commercial Inn', the 'Crown Inn' sat on the western side of the Great North Road. George Stocker was landlord from the 1920s until he retired aged nearly ninety in the 1970s. When he retired, the pub was de-licensed and became the home of his daughter and her husband. The A1 dual carriageway now passes right outside the house.

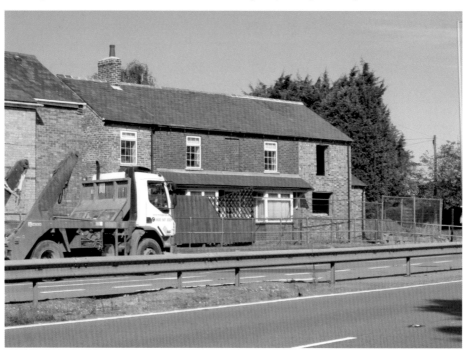

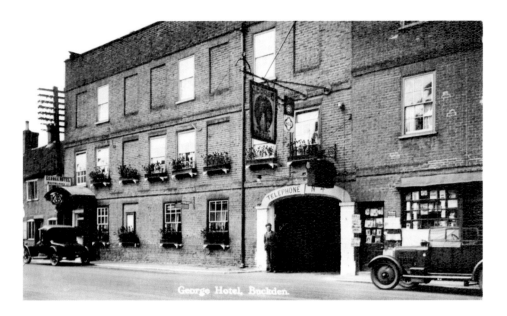

George Hotel, Buckden.

The George – Buckden

Formerly 'The George and Dragon', 'The George' is a former coaching inn built during the late 1600s – some of the timber framing has the date 1688 carved on it. The first written reference to 'The George' appears in churchwardens' accounts from 1662. The tall brick façade was added in the eighteenth century. It was famous at one time for its 'vast size and elaborate arrangements'. As coaching declined it became more popular with motor car drivers due to the inn's three on-site garages. 'The George' was bought by the Anne Furbank Group in 2003, after which it was refurbished and opened as 'The George Brasserie'.

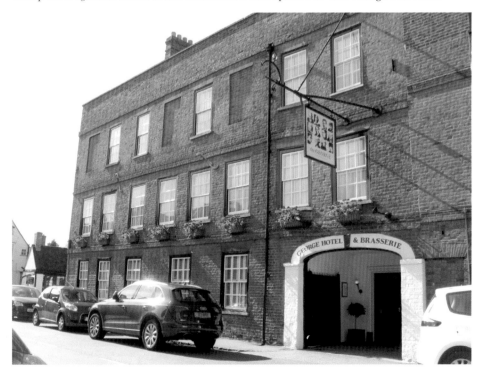

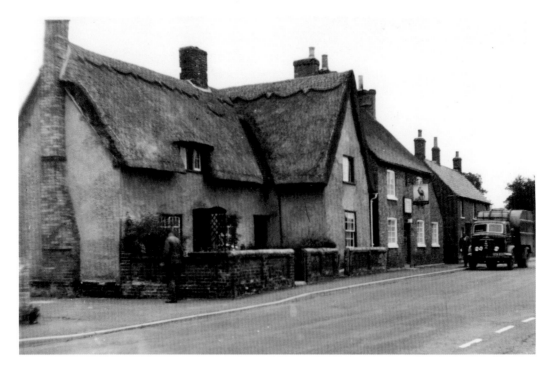

The Falcon – Mill Road, Buckden

This was the second pub in the village with this name – the first was in the High Street. It gave its name to the nearby Falcon Way. 'The Falcon' closed in October 1995 and is now a private dwelling called Crown Cottage. The thatched building next door, which can be seen in the old photograph, has been demolished.

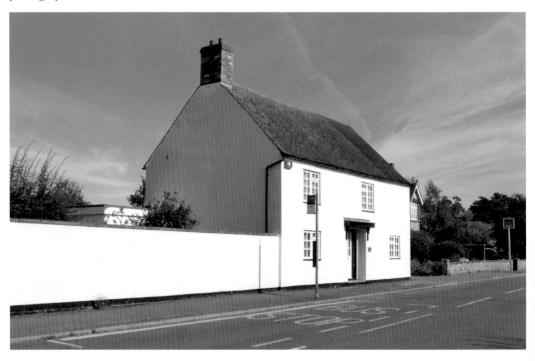

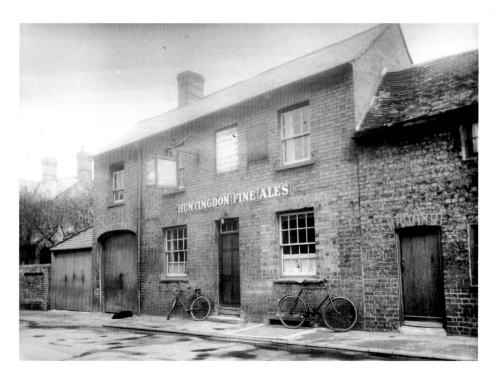

The Plough – Montagu Street, Eynesbury

'The Plough' overlooks the area around the green which was the centre of the medieval village of Eynesbury. Also in this area was the skin yard where sheepskins were used to make high quality parchment. The Plough had a brewery, bake house, stable and pigsty. It is still a pub.

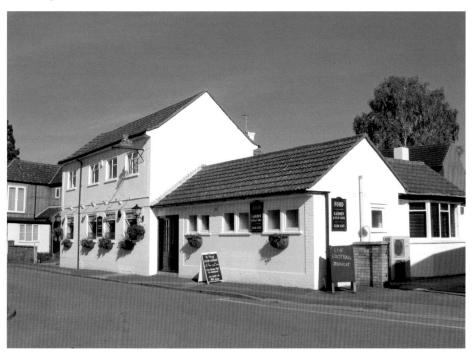

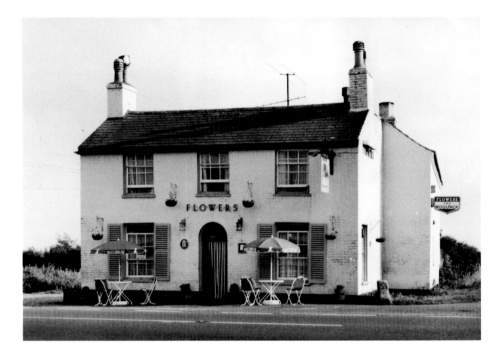

The Woolpack – Fenstanton

'The Woolpack' was situated at what became known as 'Woolpack Junction' on the crossroads of the St Ives to Biggleswade and Cambridge to Huntingdon roads. 'The Woolpack' was the subject of a compulsory purchase order in the late 1960s when the Cambridge to Huntingdon road was widened. It was demolished and the area now forms part of the Galley Hill junction of the St Ives road with the A14.

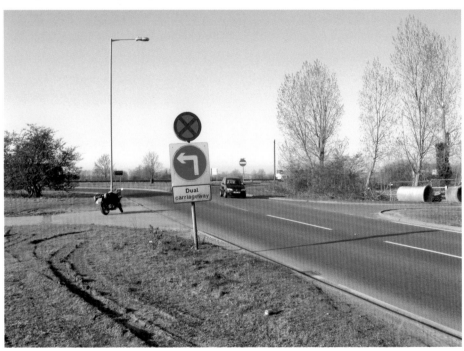

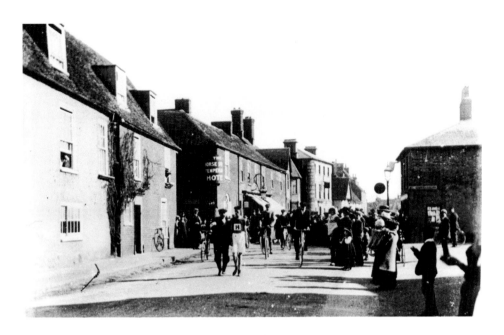

Temperance Hotel – The Causeway, Godmanchester

Originally called 'The Horseshoe Inn', by 1840 it was the principal inn in Godmanchester. In 1907 it relinquished its licence and briefly became 'The Temperance Hotel'. The Temperance movement aimed to save people, mainly the working class and children, from the evils of alcohol. Many non-conformists were supporters of the Temperance movement and Godmanchester had a particularly large group. However, the project was not a success and the hotel closed. The building became a lodging house. Today it is occupied by Gatehouse Estate Agent's. The building in the foreground of the old photograph has been demolished.

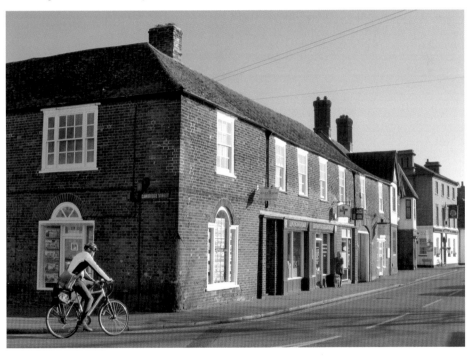

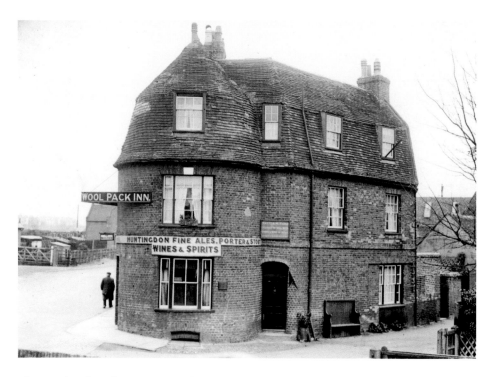

The Woolpack – The Avenue, Godmanchester

The building is dated 1801. 'The Woolpack' is situated on the Godmanchester side of the medieval bridge over the River Ouse. This area would have been busy in the days when there were two mills operating nearby. 'The Woolpack' was probably a shop before it became a pub. It was licensed in the mid-nineteenth century and the licensee was W. Rayner, a wool sorter and fell monger. The building has also been used as staff accommodation for the nearby 'Old Bridge Hotel'.

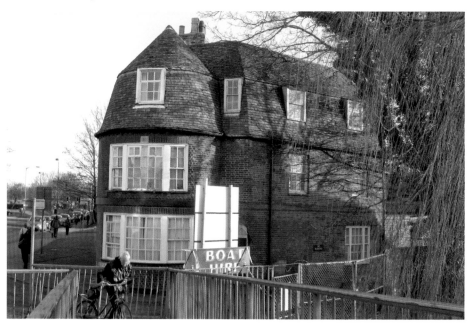

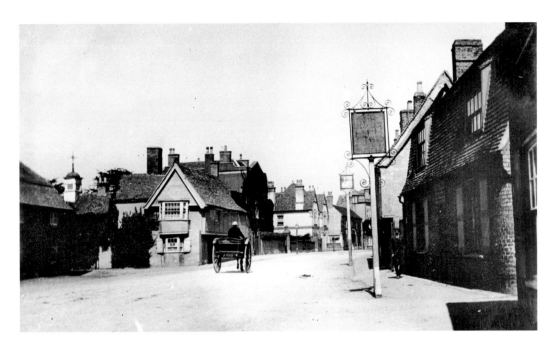

The Rose and Crown – Post Street, Godmanchester

'The Rose and Crown' was one of several pubs along Post Street. By 1940 the licensee was Mrs Lucy Hilsden who was Godmanchester's first female mayor. Being unable to ride, she was the first mayor of Godnmanchester to break the centuries-old tradition of reading the proclamation of a new monarch's reign from horseback. 'The Rose and Crown' ceased to be a pub in 1965. The premises are now a place of worship, a Meeting House used by the Society of Friends, commonly known as Quakers.

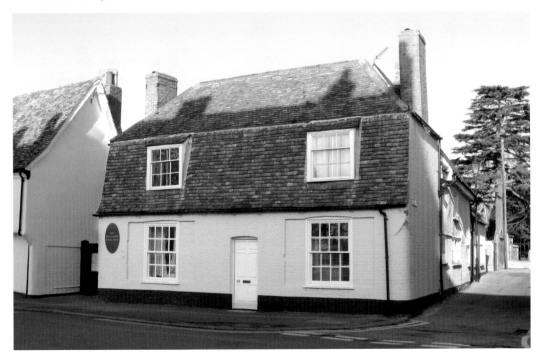

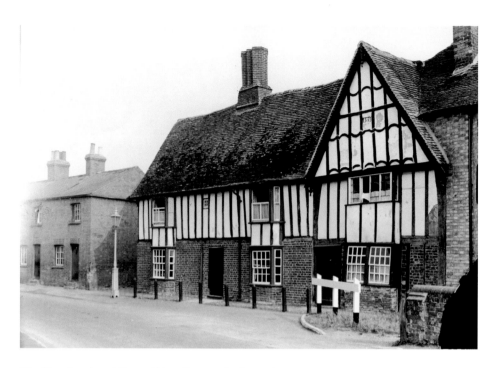

The Shepherd and Dog – West Street, Godmanchester

'The Shepherd and Dog' allegedly dates back to 1593 according to the inscription on the building. According to Godmanchester historian F. W. Bird, the first tenant of this beerhouse was William Reed, 'a gentle shepherd'. Only No. 31 was once the beerhouse; the present building is known as 'Shepherd's Halt' and comprises both No. 31 and No. 32 West Street which was originally a separate dwelling to the west.

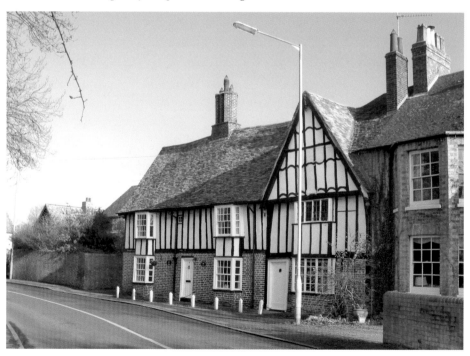

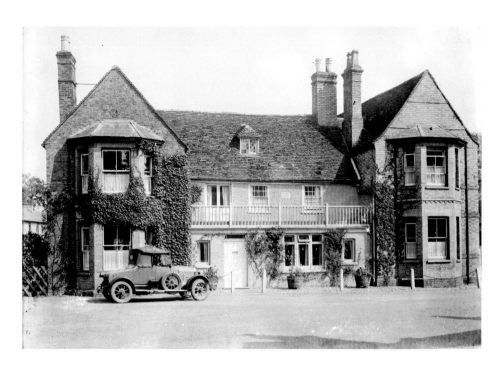

The Black Bull – Post Street, Godmanchester

'The Black Bull' is Grade II listed. The timber framed section probably dates to the seventeenth century. In the days when tolls were charged for carts crossing the bridge into Huntingdon, 'The Black Bull' offered stabling for farmers who then walked over the bridge and avoided the tolls. In the early twentieth century, 'The Black Bull' became 'Avenue House', a private hotel, where Mrs George offered 'every comfort, homemade cakes and scones, teas and coffee and a motor garage'. When 'The Railway Inn' closed, the license was transferred to 'The Black Bull' and it became a pub again.

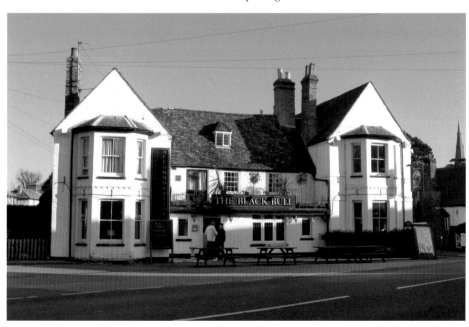

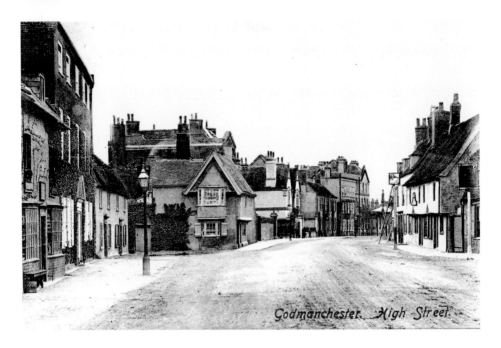

The (White) Swan – Post Street, Godmanchester

This was situated next door to the 'Rose and Crown' pub. Pevsner dates the 'Swan' or 'White Swan' to the seventeenth century. At one time, it brewed its own beer, which was popular with the bargemen and watermen due to the inn's proximity to Mill Yard (now a car park). The property was restored in 1986 and is now called Hatton House – possibly after Elizabeth's courtier Sir Christopher Hatton who is supposed to have given it to his nephew.

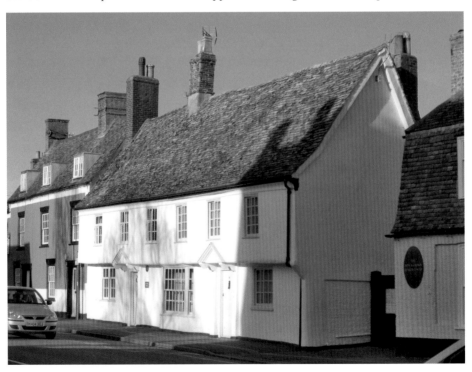

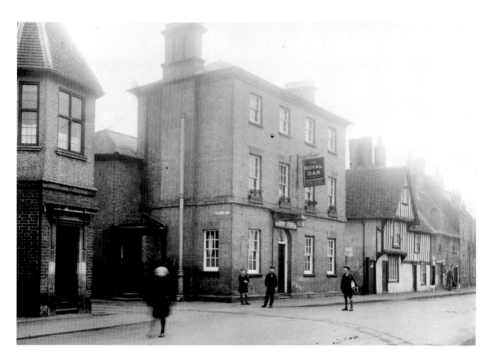

The Royal Oak – The Causeway, Godmanchester

'The Royal Oak' is a Grade II listed building. It was built of Gault brick (a yellowish white colour brick popular in Victorian times) around 1840. It is still a pub and looks very little changed except that the lower storey is now painted white. A long established bowling green behind the pub is still in use by the Royal Oak Bowls Club.

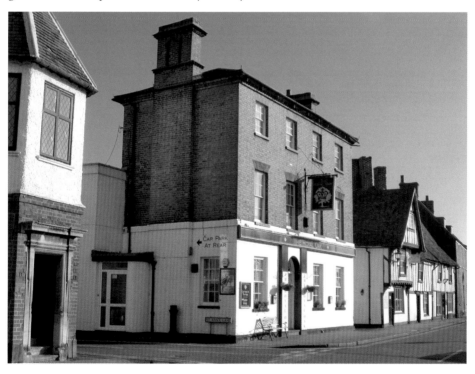

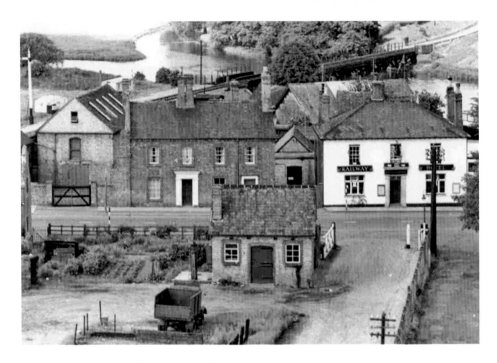

The Railway Inn – Bridge Place, Godmanchester

'The Railway Inn' or 'Tavern' was so named because it stood next to Godmanchester Station which was on the old Cambridge line. The railway line closed to passengers in 1959 and the pub followed soon after, closing in the 1960s. Almost all traces of the railway line and the station have disappeared and it is hard to imagine it was ever there. The building was bypassed when the road was diverted to pass under the A14 flyover and now sits in a cul-de-sac next to an electricity sub-station.

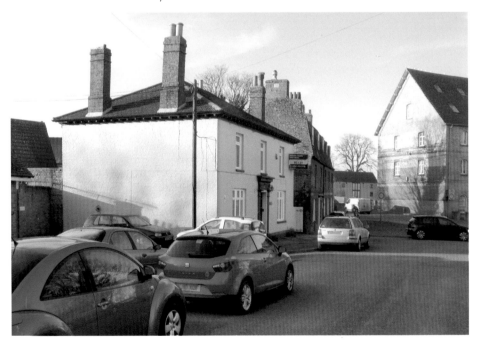

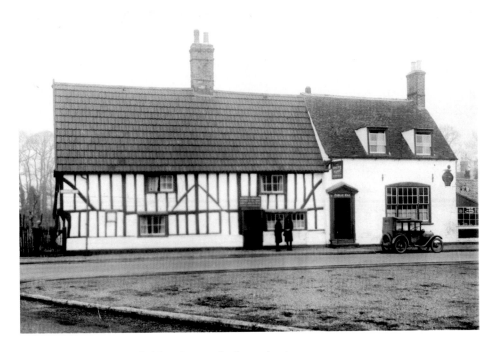

The White Hart – Cambridge Street, Godmanchester

'The White Hart' is one of many fine seventeenth-century buildings with exposed timber framing that survive in Godmanchester. 'The White Hart' was the livery badge of King Richard II (1377-99) who introduced legislation compelling public houses to display a sign in order to facilitate the collection of tax. The name 'White Hart' became so common that it was at one time almost synonymous with public houses. 'The White Hart' in Godmanchester has been refurbished and is still trading as a pub and restaurant.

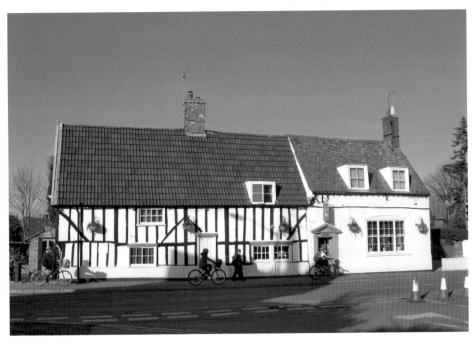

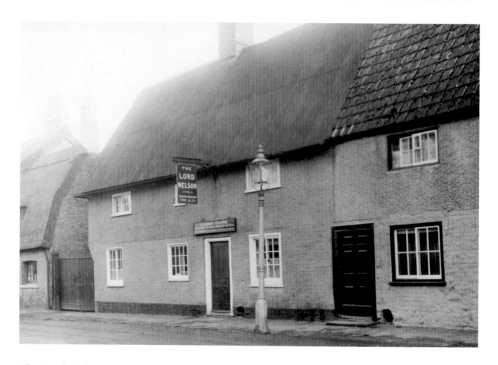

The Lord Nelson – West Street, Godmanchester

'The Lord Nelson' was originally a thatched building but subsequently had a tin roof. It was obviously a family friendly place as it also had a small sweet shop! The pub closed in the mid-1950s and the building was advertised for sale in 1959 in *The Hunts Post* and sold for £700. At this time it had no gas or electricity and was lit by candles, according to Bert Brudenell who bought it.

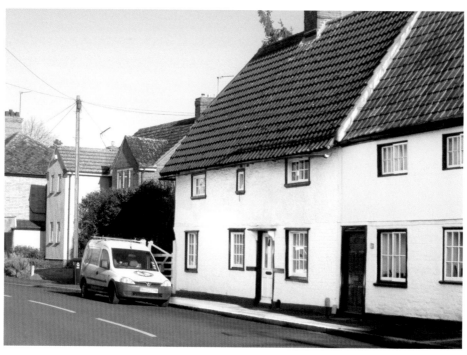

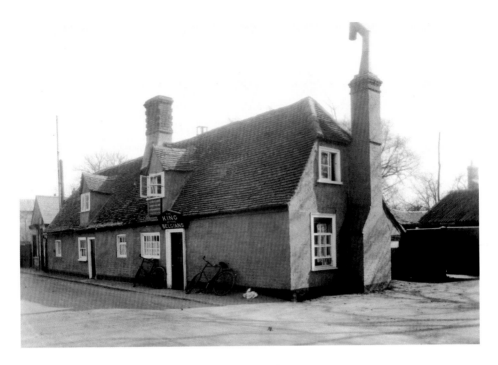

The King of the Belgians – Main Street, Hartford

This ancient pub was said to have been a drinking place of Oliver Cromwell. Built in 1541, it has been a pub for over 450 years. It was originally called 'The King of Prussia' but changed its name to something less Germanic during the First World War. In 2005, plans to turn it in to a private house were opposed by local people and rejected by the Council, so it remained a pub. The modern photograph is an interior view of the main bar.

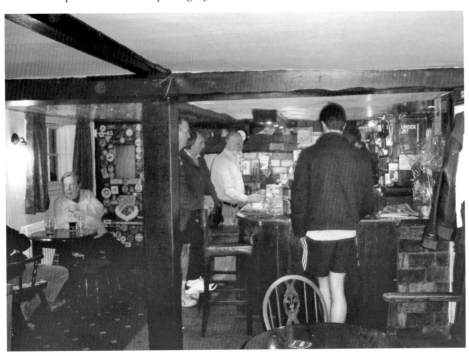

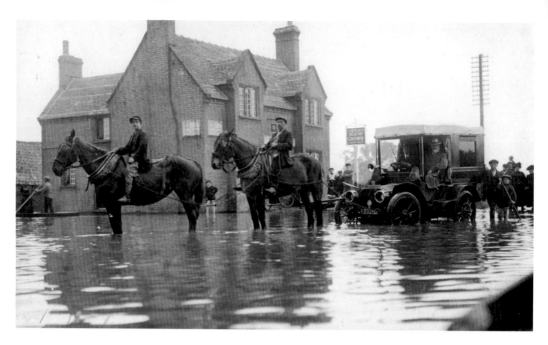

The New Crown – Hemingford

'The New Crown' stood on the corner of London Road and Hemingford Road on what is now known as Armes Corner. It was named after James Armes, a publican of 'The New Crown'. The old photograph was taken during the floods of August 1912. Two horses have been hitched to a motor car to pull it out of the water. The pub closed in 1967 and is now a private house.

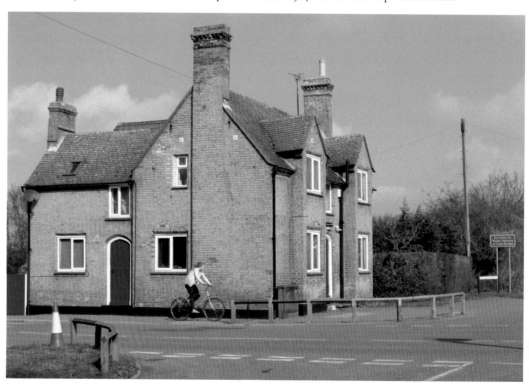

The Bell – St Germain Street, Huntingdon

One of several pubs in St Germain Street that was, at one time, the principal road into Huntingdon. In 1901, *The Hunts Post* reported that a cow being driven up St Germain Street strolled 'in the front door of 'The Bell Public House'...it made for the parlour bar – no damage was done'. The newer photograph shows 'The Bell' during the 1970s. By then many of the houses in St Germain Street had been lost during the town development. The whole street disappeared during the redevelopment of Chequers Court and the building of St Germain Walk in 1999.

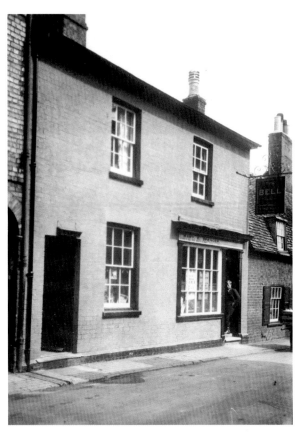

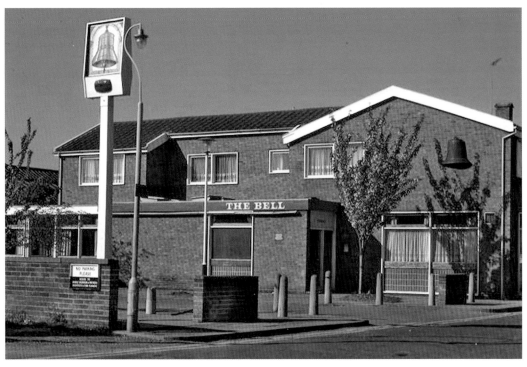

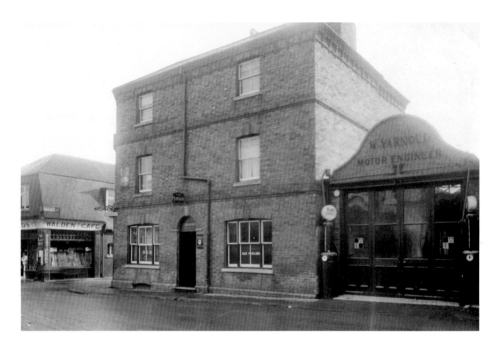

The Swan – George Street, Huntingdon

The pub was built in 1839 on land belonging to the Earl of Sandwich. The landlords held a variety of other jobs – coach painter, shepherd and coal merchant. In the late eighteenth century they began to specialise in hiring out ponies and traps. By 1909, motor cars were also available for hire. Soon the business had expanded to include buying, selling and repairing cars, probably from the adjacent building. The pub closed in 1964. The small building on the right is now part of Elphicks which has been in business next door since 1911.

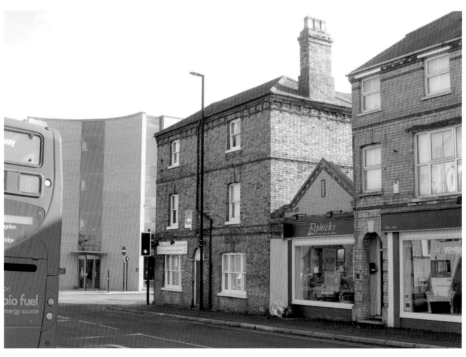

The Market Inn – Huntingdon

'The Market Inn' is one of Huntingdon's oldest buildings. It has been a pub for about 400 years. George Ashpole, landlord of 'The Market Inn' from 1932, had been awarded the Military Medal at Passchaendaele, and in 1944 he was awarded the MBE for services to the Home Guard which he joined on the day it was formed. Sadly, he died in 1947 aged just fifty-three. 'The Market Inn' is a half-timbered building retaining some original internal features. It is still a pub, almost hidden from sight behind the town hall.

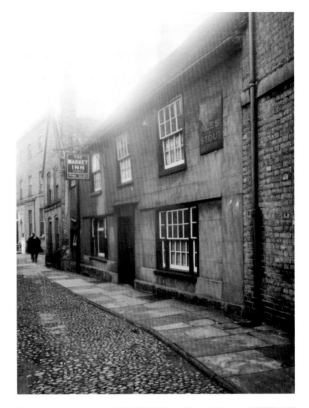

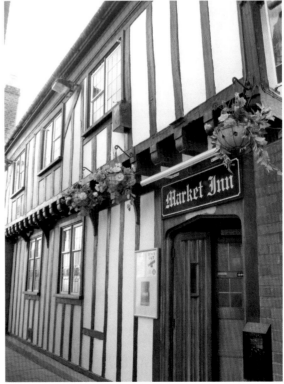

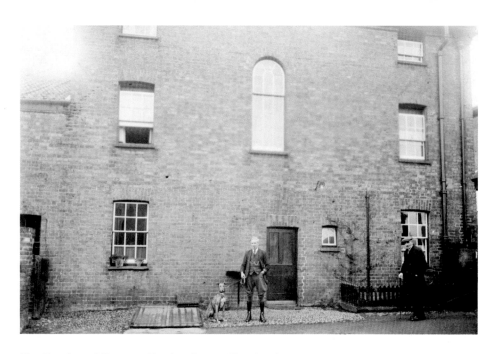

The Coach and Horses – Ermine Street, Huntingdon

'The Coach and Horses' is first mentioned as a pub in 1799. Records show that in March 1858, the landlord George Radwell was charged with selling beer on a Sunday after a woman was seen leaving the premises with beer bottles. Charges were dropped when it was revealed that a serving girl had been taking the beer to sick prisoners at the nearby goal in St Peter's Road whilst Radwell and his wife were at church. The premises are now home to the 'Raj Vujon Indian Restaurant' with 'The Coach and Horses B&B' next door.

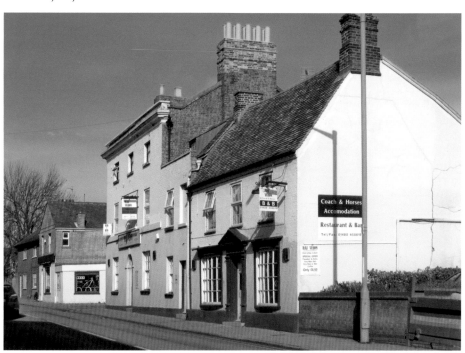

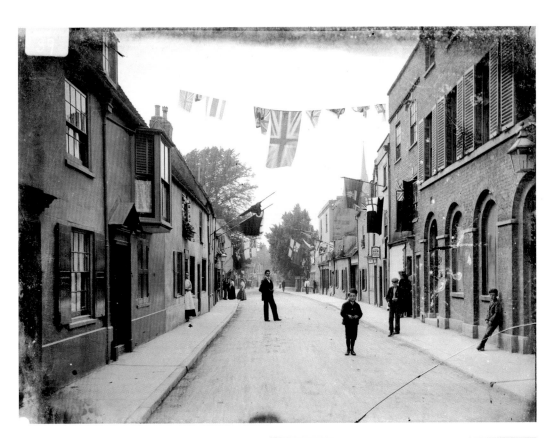

The Duke of Cumberland – High Street, Huntingdon

'The Duke of Cumberland' is on the left of this scene from Queen Victoria's Diamond Jubilee. The best known Duke of Cumberland was Prince William, younger son of George II, notorious for crushing the Jacobite rebellion after the Battle of Culloden in 1746. The pub was closed down in 1916 because it was 'not required for public convenience', being one of three licensed premises within 46 yards ('The Waterloo' remained open and 'The Red Lion' was also closed). In the borough as a whole there was one pub for every 138 people. The building is now empty.

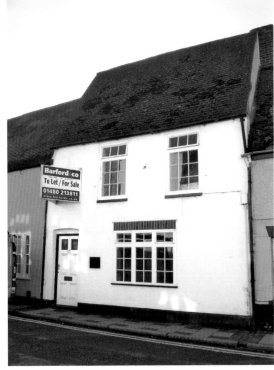

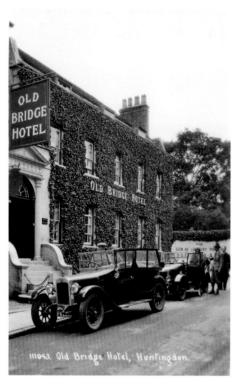

Old Bridge Hotel – Huntingdon

The 'Old Bridge' was originally built during the Georgian period as a private house. In the early 1900s, it was purchased by the Country Motoring Club for use as the Club's Huntingdon HQ and clubrooms. By 1915, it changed hands again and became a hotel. During the First World War it became the local headquarters of the Royal Flying Corps which had an airfield at Portholme. It is still trading and is little changed in appearance.

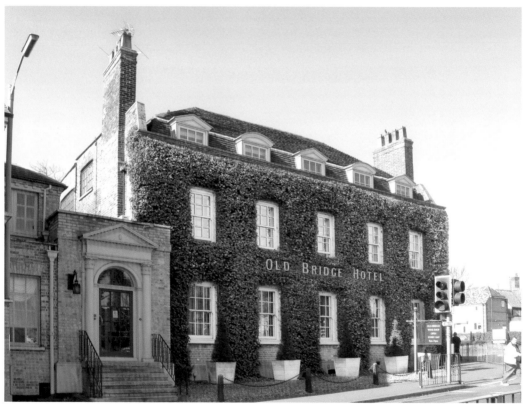

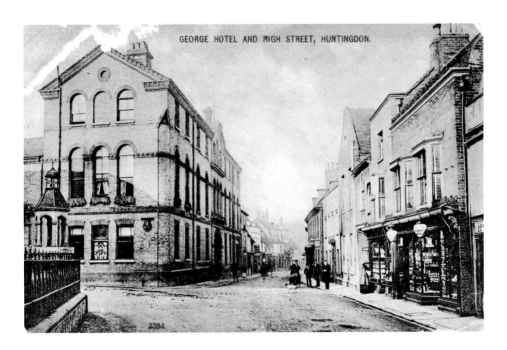

GEORGE HOTEL AND HIGH STREET, HUNTINGDON.

The George (1) – High Street, Huntingdon

'The George' is first mentioned in the 1572 borough survey and was at one time the most important of Huntingdon's inns. Charles I used it as his headquarters when the Royalist army occupied the town in 1645 and the Duke of Manchester also used it as a meeting point for his 'light horse' mounted volunteer brigade. The grand façade facing the street was designed by Robert Hutchinson. It was built in 1865 after a disastrous fire destroyed much of the original building. The building has changed very little since then.

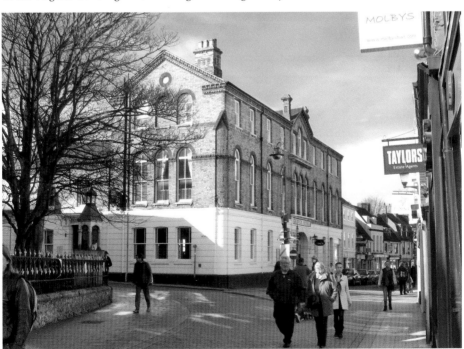

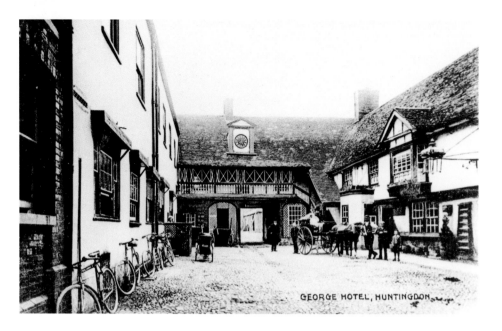

The George (2) – Huntingdon

'The George' courtyard is the oldest part of the building. It still has two sides of its seventeenth-century courtyard and open gallery which escaped the fire of 1865. 'The George' only really took off with the coming of the coach trade. A two-storey stable block was added in the early eighteenth century. In the 1820s, the yard would have been bustling, with four coaches a day leaving 'The George' for London. These pictures show a slightly more sedate scene.

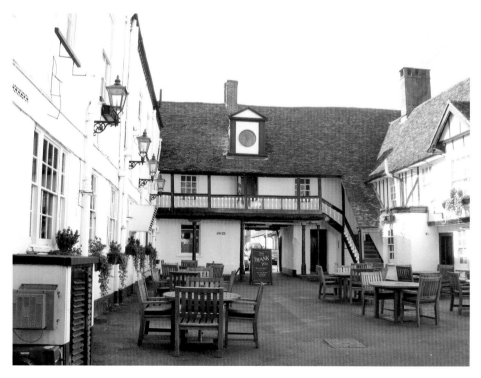

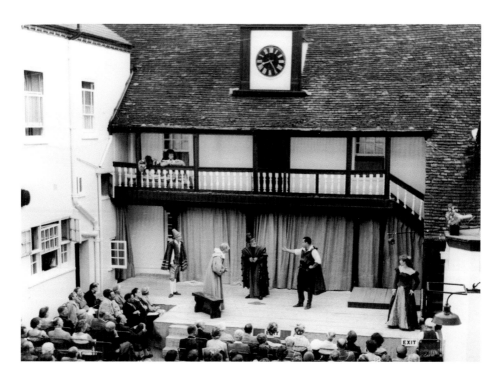

The George (3) – Huntingdon

'The George' has a long history of staging plays – they were held here before the theatre was built on the corner of George Street in 1801.

The tradition was revived in 1959 with a production of Shakespeare's *Taming of the Shrew*. Productions of Shakespeare's plays have been held in the courtyard ever since and annually since 1978. The productions are run by a group of trustees and the entire cast and crew are volunteers. The modern photograph is of the 2011 production of *Measure for Measure* and is reproduced by the kind permission of Antonia Brown, official photographer for 'Shakespeare at The George'.

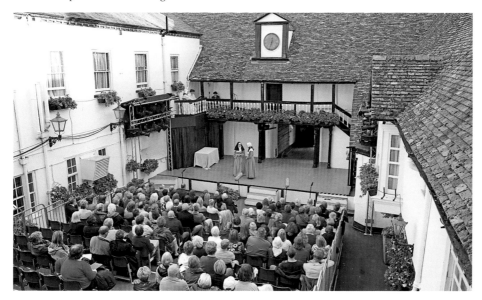

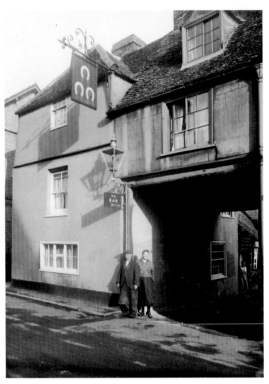

**The Three Horseshoes –
St John's Street, Huntingdon**

A beerhouse on the corner of Royal Oak
Passage. Three horseshoes is the heraldic
sign of the Worshipful Company of
Farriers. Whenever a pub takes the name,
it is an indicator that a blacksmith or
farrier was nearby. Here, in the 1870s, the
landlord John Peel combined both trades.
A horseshoes sign was also popular
because it had the reputation of being
able to combat witchcraft and bring
good luck. The licence of 'The Three
Horseshoes' lapsed in 1935 and the site
has been redeveloped into flats.

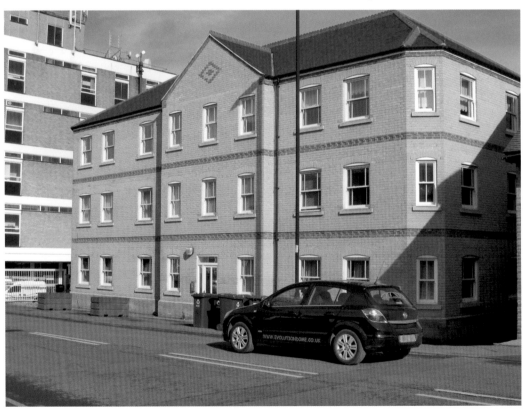

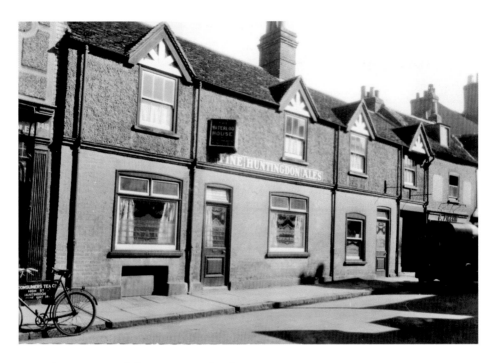

Waterloo House – High Street, Huntingdon

Previously called 'The Horse and Jockey', it probably changed its name soon after the Battle of Waterloo in 1815 where the Duke of Wellington finally defeated Napoleon Bonaparte. According to an 1860 sale brochure, as well as the usual bars, the pub had 'six sleeping rooms with convenient closets and cupboards' as well as a dairy, two brew houses, a pigsty and a well of water. Six hundred gallons of 'excellent ale' were sold separately. The pub later became O'Reilly's and is now the Samuel Pepys Diary Rooms.

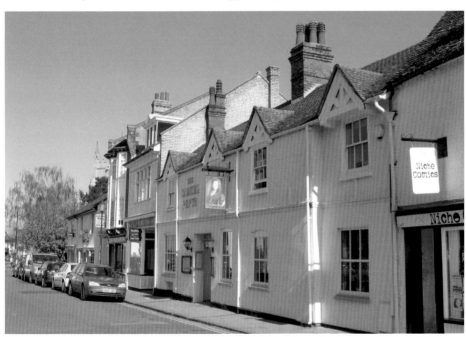

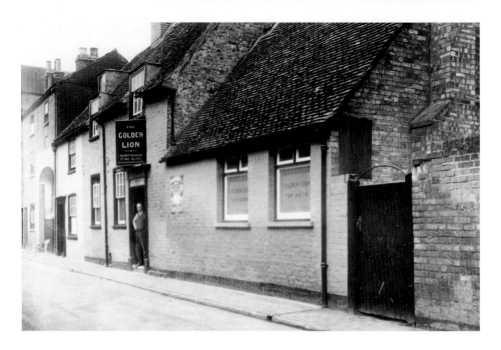

The Golden Lion – St Germain Street, Huntingdon

Records show that 'The Golden Lion' was frequently involved in cases of drunkenness, such as in 1903 when one Guy Riseley was found outside in the street, his face covered with blood. He was so drunk he had to be carried to the police station in a wheelbarrow. The landlord often found himself in trouble for allowing drunken behaviour, but you have to feel some sympathy; in 1909 Frederick Jarrett was charged with drunkenness, but claimed that the law did not apply to him because he was a Welshman. St Germain Street has been replaced with St Germain Walk.

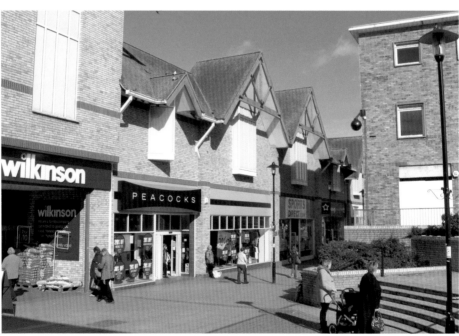

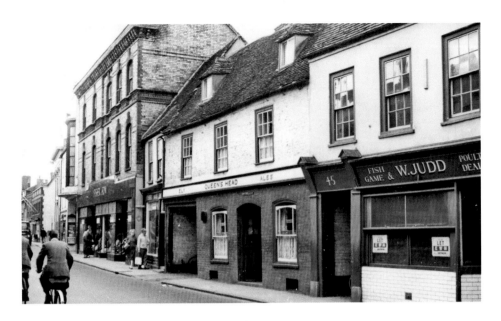

The Queen's Head – High Street, Huntingdon

This pub stood on the corner of Queen's Head Passage. Tragedy struck there in 1928 when Violet Brattle, daughter of the landlord, disappeared on the eve of her wedding to Charles Spencer, son of the landlord of 'The Bell' in St Germain Street. Three weeks later her body was found in the River Ouse. The inquest recorded a verdict of 'suicide whilst temporarily insane' when it was revealed that she had been worried about moving to Poole. The former Queen's Head Passage is now nothing but a yard. The pub building still remains and is now Santander Bank.

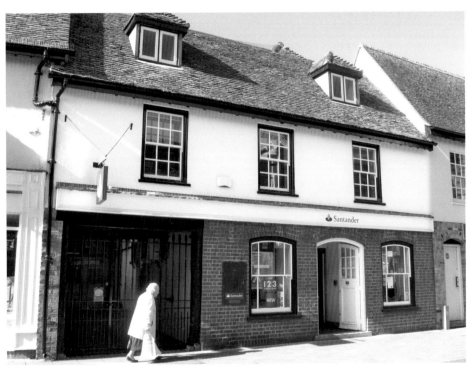

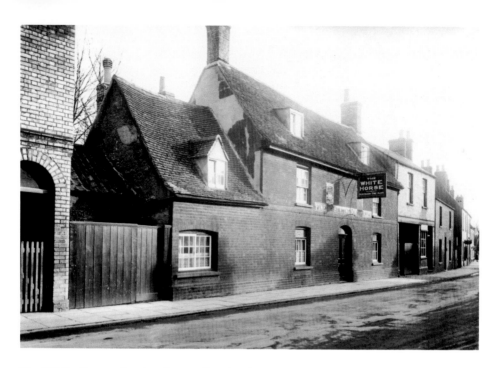

The White Horse – Ermine Street, Huntingdon

This has been a pub since at least the 1700s. Landlords of such establishments generally had another trade as well. John Byfield, who became landlord on 1869, was also a carpenter. Tragedy struck when he was working on the restoration of Brampton church roof in 1877. Byfield fell while cutting one of the rafters and was killed instantly. In 1964 the license was transferred to a new pub with a larger catchment area, 'The Lord Protector' on the new Oxmoor estate. The building was demolished and is now part of the Great Northern Street car park next to Lloyds Pharmacy.

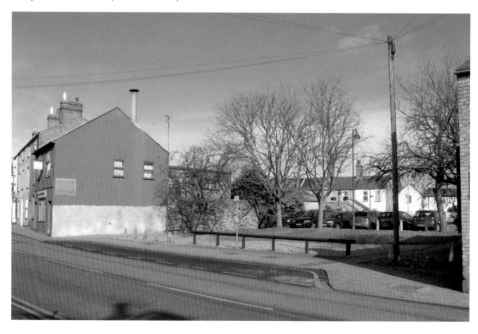

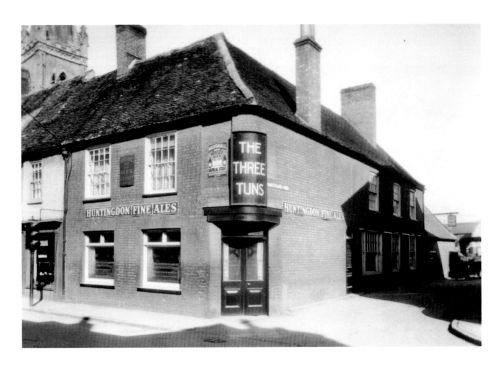

The Three Tuns – High Street, Huntingdon

The junction of Hartford Road and the High Street has seen many changes. In 1572 this was the site of the town prison. Opposite was St Mary's Vicarage, demolished in 1937 to widen a dangerous corner. Marshall's garage (formerly Maddox and Kirby) which replaced it was itself later demolished. 'The Three Tuns' survived despite being damaged in 1882 by a fire caused by a lighted pipe being left in a coat pocket in one of the bedrooms. It was briefly renamed 'The Dog and Bone' in the 1990s but has now reverted to its former name.

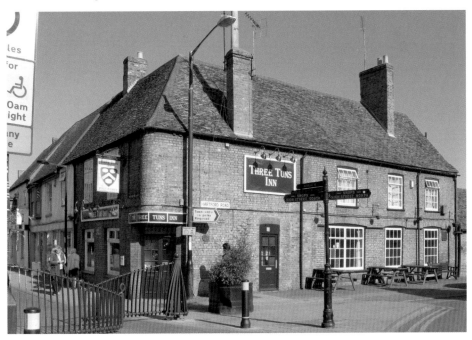

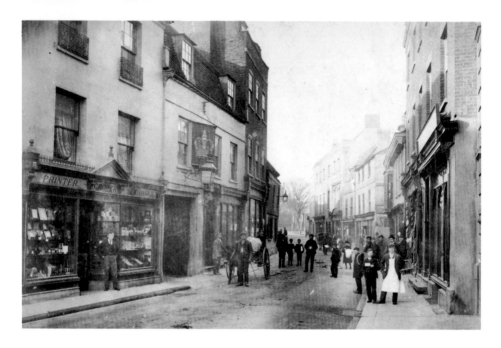

The Crown Hotel – High Street, Huntingdon

'The Crown Hotel' was established in 1765. An advert of 1858 claimed it had 'well-aired beds, loose boxes and lock up coach houses. Wines and spirits of the best quality, home brewed and Burton Ale, London Porter etc.' In 1912, the license was relinquished and the property was sold for £800. The whole building was rebuilt and by 1940 it housed the offices of the Inland Revenue. By 1963, the building was the office of Pearl Assurance. It is now the Carphone Warehouse.

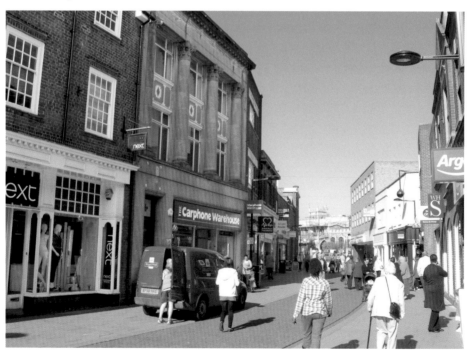

The Bull – High Street, Huntingdon

Huntingdonshire had a fearsome reputation for highway robbery among travellers during the eighteenth and nineteenth centuries. 'The Bull Inn' was infamous in coaching days as a resort of highwaymen, Dick Turpin amongst them. The inn's hostlers reputedly made a bit on the side by supplying information about the contents of coaches which called here. This may be legend, but Turpin is known to have been active along the Great North Road near Alconbury. 'The Bull', which was between St Mary's Churchyard and the Vicarage, later became Dilley's furniture sale rooms before being demolished. It now forms part of Saxongate.

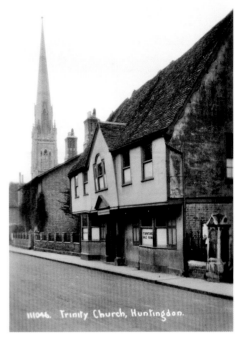

11046. Trinity Church, Huntingdon.

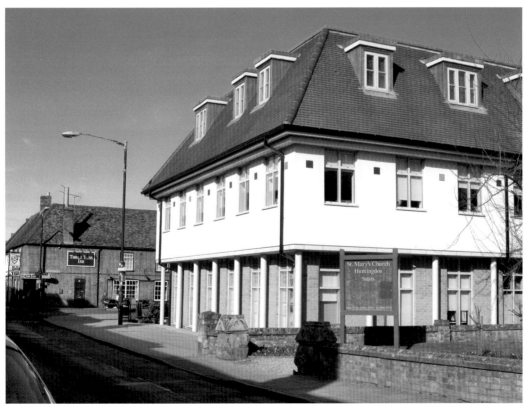

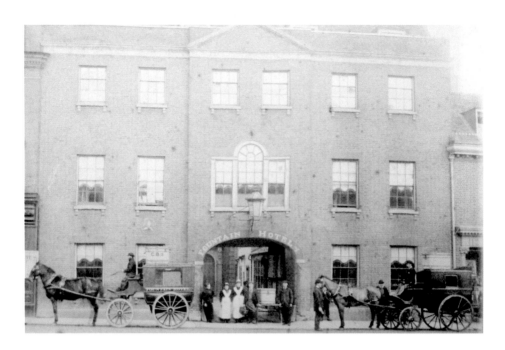

The Fountain (1) – Market Square, Huntingdon

During the eighteenth century two coaches, the *Boston Mail* and the *Edinburgh Mail,* left for London each day from 'The Fountain'. As well as ale, food and rooms for travellers the inn offered entertainment too. Cock fights were held here, including, in July 1800, a match between 'the gentlemen of Huntingdonshire' and those of Warwickshire. 'The Fountain' became Murkett Brothers' garage in 1911. The old Corn Exchange, behind the inn was converted into the Grand Cinema which opened in 1912. In the 1960s, Murkett Brothers' garage moved to new premises and 'The Fountain' was put up for sale.

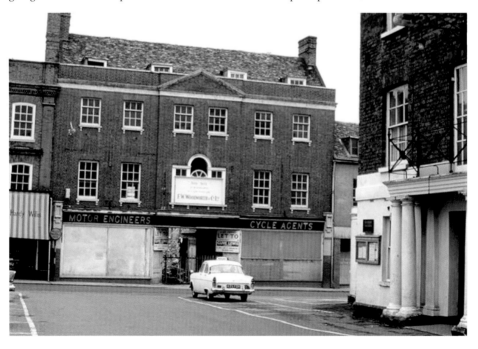

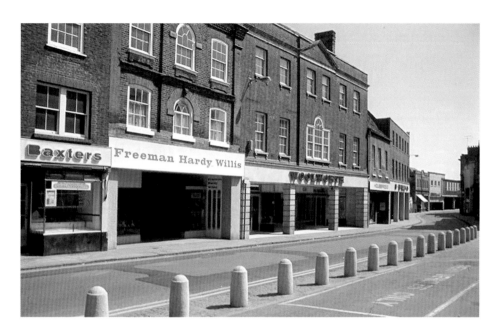

The Fountain (2) – Market Square, Huntingdon

When Murketts sold the site it was purchased by F. W. Woolworth's. The old Woolworth's store had been opposite in what is now 'The Bright House.' The yard was incorporated into the sales area and the large new Woolworth's store opened in 1969 selling a variety of goods including frozen food, fresh fruit and vegetables. After trading for forty years the company folded and the Huntingdon branch of Woolworth's closed in January 2009. This historic Georgian building is now home to the 99p store.

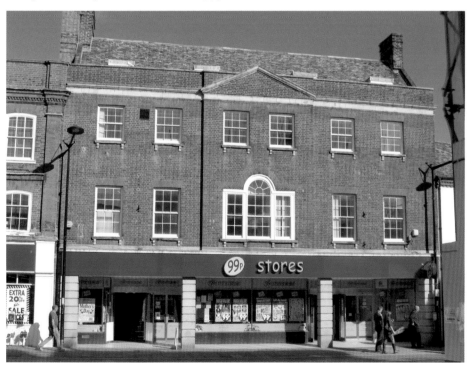

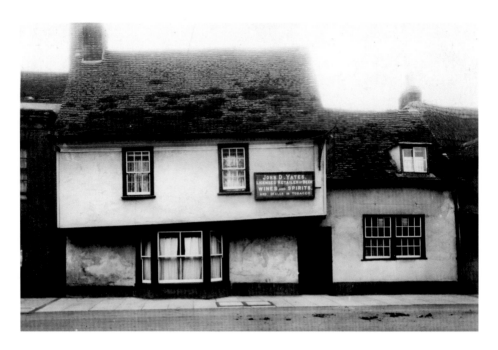

The Rose and Crown – High Street, Ramsey

'The Rose and Crown' was one of the few seventeenth century buildings left in Ramsey after a series of fires. However, by the 1970s, it had been demolished and the area was being used as a car park. It was earmarked for a shopping development in the 1978 local plan. This obviously came to nothing, however, as the area is now a housing area named Crown Mews.

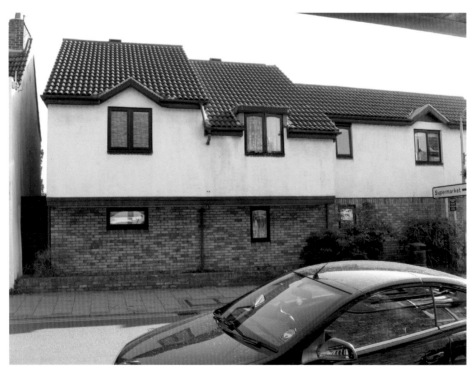

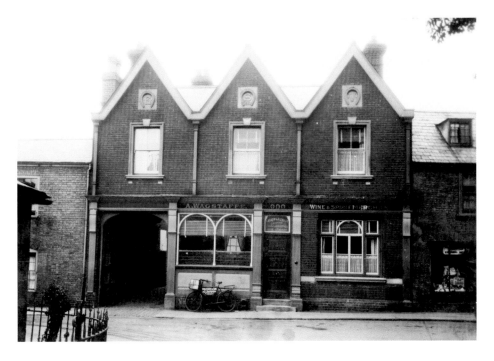

The Three Horseshoes – Little Whyte, Ramsey

During the early 1900s 'The Three Horseshoes' was run by Edward Venimore Sewell who was also in business as a miller (both wind and steam), not a blacksmith as you might expect. Why were pubs named three horseshoes rather than four? It is said this is because the horse stood on three shoes whilst being shod. 'The Three Horseshoes' is still in business today.

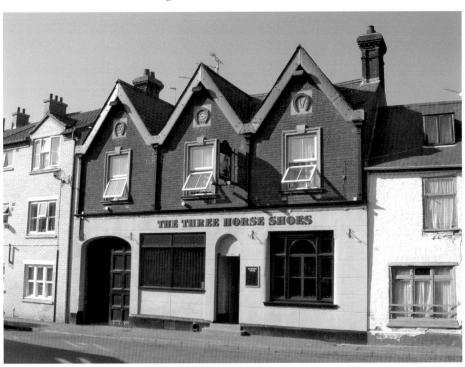

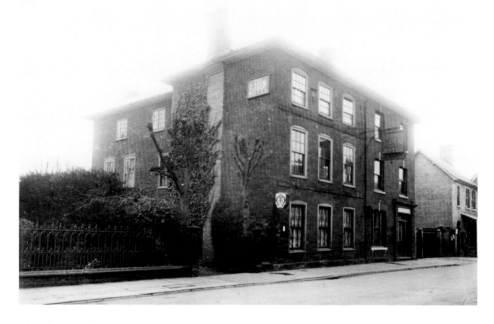

The Lion Hotel – High Street, Ramsey

'The Lion' is dated 1731. In its heyday it had an impressive lounge on the ground floor where large groups of farmers were served by waitresses carrying drinks through from the public bar. Bedrooms on the upper floor led into one another so visitors might pass through two or three other rooms to reach their own. The middle floor had a grand piano. 'The Lion' closed in 1989 and was converted into flats.

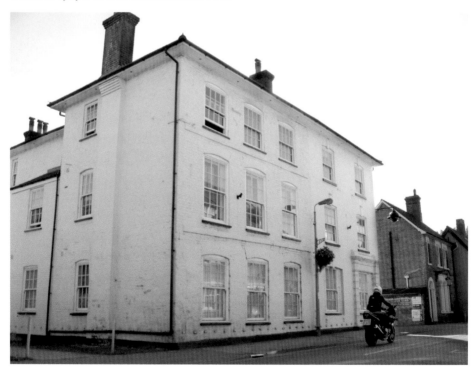

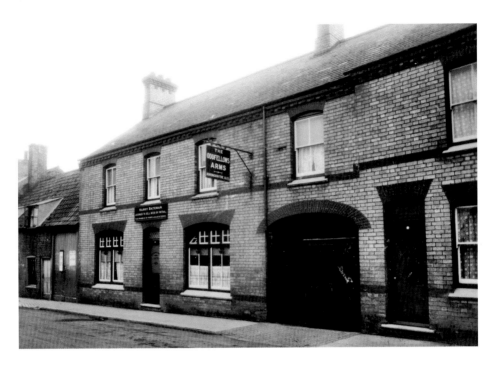

The Oddfellows Arms – High Street, Ramsey

The term 'Odd Fellows' comes from the fact that in smaller towns there were too few fellows in the same trade to form a local guild. Men from several trades, therefore, joined together to form a local guild of fellows from different trades, named the 'Odd Fellows'. Many pubs in Britain are named 'The Oddfellows Arms', probably because they were once meeting places of these groups. The former 'Oddfellows Arms' in Ramsey is now a private house.

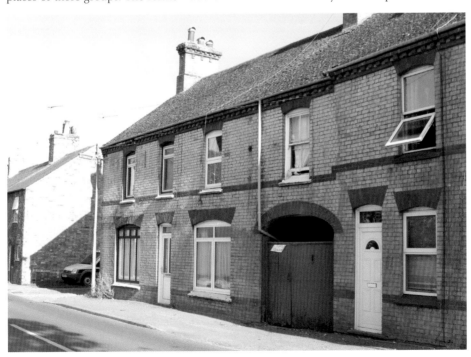

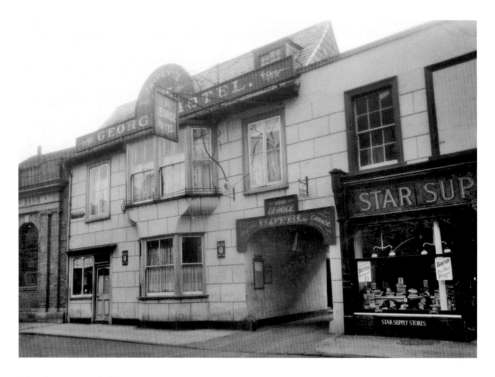

The George – High Street, Ramsey

Formerly known as 'The George and Dragon', this is of the few remaining buildings in Ramsey with seventeenth-century features. It survived a devastating fire in 1731, which burnt for several days and destroyed more than eighty houses on the north side of the High Street and the west of Great Whyte, as well as granaries full of malt and wheat. The façade was rebuilt in the nineteenth century. It is still a hotel.

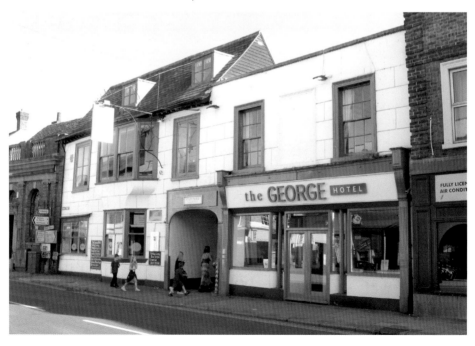

**The George Yard –
High Street, Ramsey**
The old picture is an
1888 engraving by John
Poulter. The ladder on
the right leads up to the
hay loft and there are
pigeons flying down to
look for spilled corn.
The yard is the oldest
part of the George, with
parts of it including the
staircase dating from the
seventeenth century.

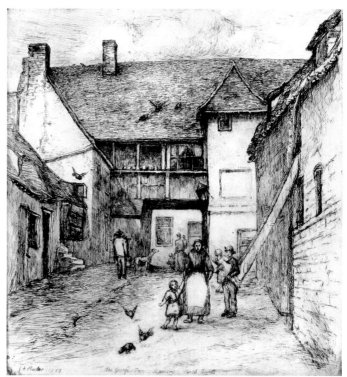

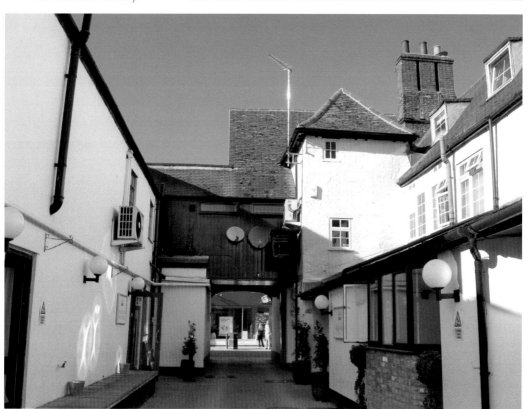

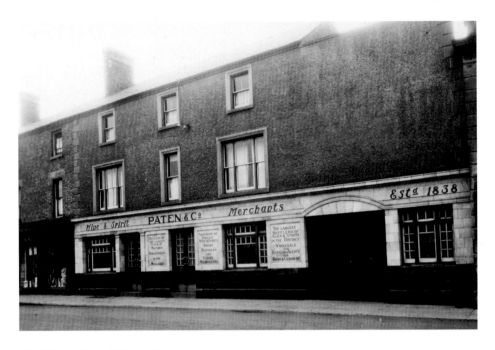

The Vine – Great Whyte, Ramsey

'The Vine' was one of as many as eighteen pubs that lined the Great Whyte, which included 'The Recruiting Sergeant', 'The Spotted Dog', 'The Seven Stars' and many more. It was owned by Paten & Co. wine and spirit merchants and bottlers of Peterborough. The building was pulled down around 1970 and was replaced by a supermarket. It has been variously Safeway, then Somerfield and Haldanes. It is currently a factory outlet shop.

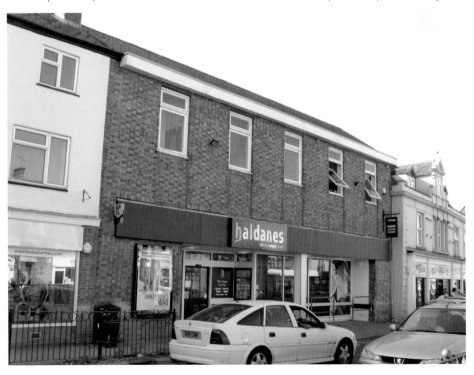

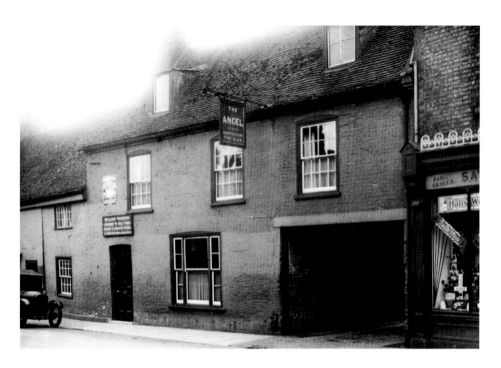

The Angel – High Street, Ramsey

Religious symbols are quite common on pub signs and may date from the days when many early hostelries were associated with the church. Nearby Ramsey Abbey was once one of the most important religious centres in England before the Dissolution of the Monasteries. 'The Angel' is still a pub today.

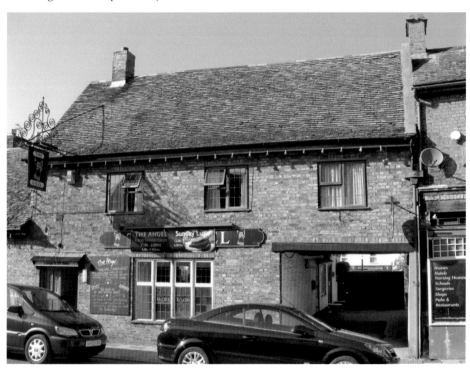

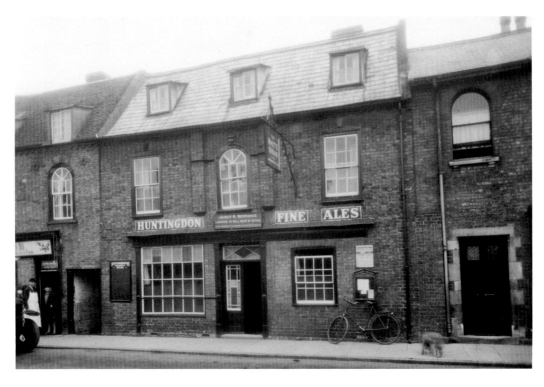

The White Swan – Great Whyte, Ramsey

When 'The White Swan' closed, the premises were purchased by Douglas Bream who already had a business in the town. In 1962, he opened a shop repairing and selling shoes at the former pub. The shop is still in business as D. W. Bream today.

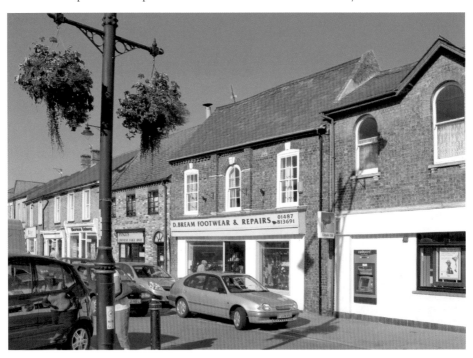

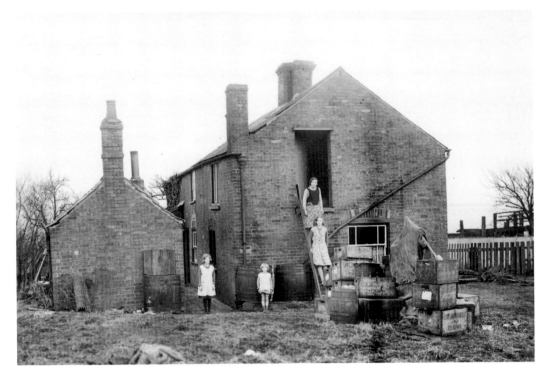

Speed the Plough – Ramsey St Mary

'Speed the Plough' beerhouse was at Raveley Drain End. When the old photograph was taken it was a free house owned by Walter Pettit. Its name suggests it was used by agricultural labourers working nearby. Before the use of farm machinery, agricultural labour was hard work and the men were allowed between 6 and 8 pints of beer or ale a day to keep up their intake of calories. The beerhouse is now Speed the Plough Farm, north of Woodwalton Nature Reserve.

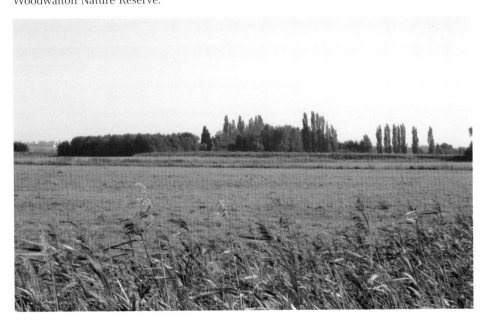

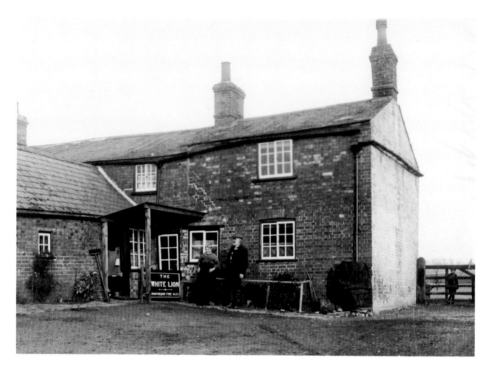

The White Lion – Ramsey St Mary

'The White Lion' is a much rarer name for a pub than 'The Red Lion'. The name symbolised courage and has been associated with both King Edward IV and King Edward VI, as well as the Duke of Norfolk. 'The White Lion' at Ramsey Herne was once a beerhouse. Nowadays it is a pub, simply called 'The Lion'.

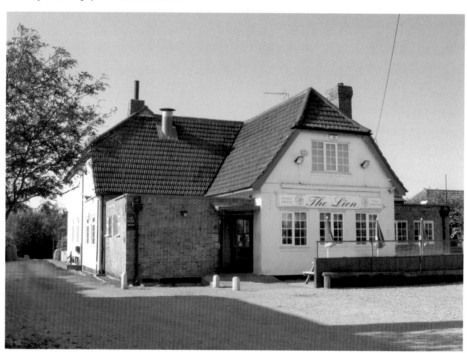

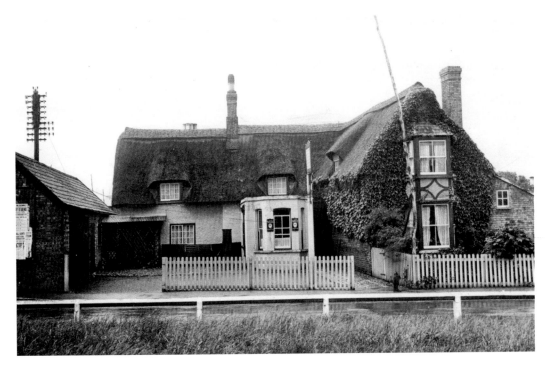

The Chequers Inn – Sawtry

'The Chequers Inn' stood opposite the Green which was the focal point of village activities, the local hunt and celebrations such as 'Feast Week'. At such times, the pub would be so busy that one local man recalls 'you could serve your own beer and leave the money on the barrel'. The building remains almost unchanged, although it is now a private house.

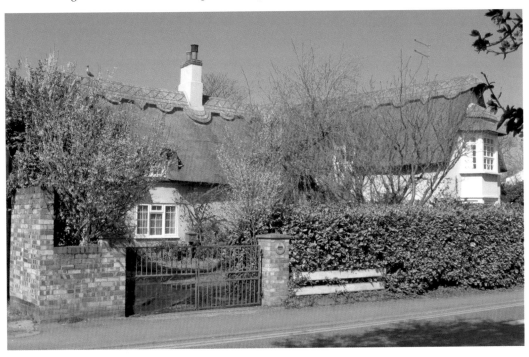

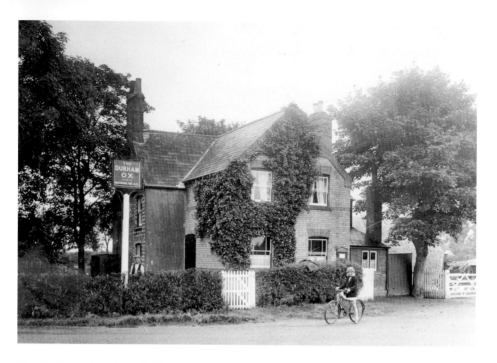

The Durham Ox – St Judith's Lane, Sawtry

'The Durham Ox' was one of a number of enormous cattle bred in County Durham. It weighed 168 stone and was sold for £140 in about 1801. The name became popular for inns and may have been chosen in Sawtry due to the proximity of the Bullock Road, used to drive sheep and cattle from the north to the London markets. The pub was known locally as 'The Bull' and the building, now a private house, remains almost unchanged. Nearby Durham Close was named after the pub.

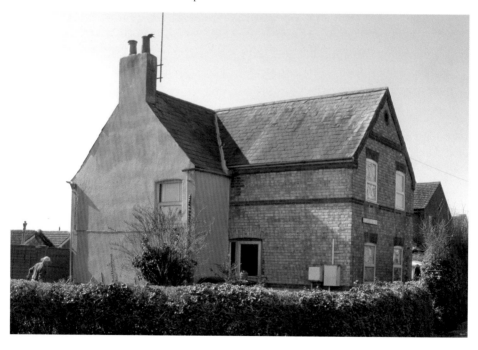

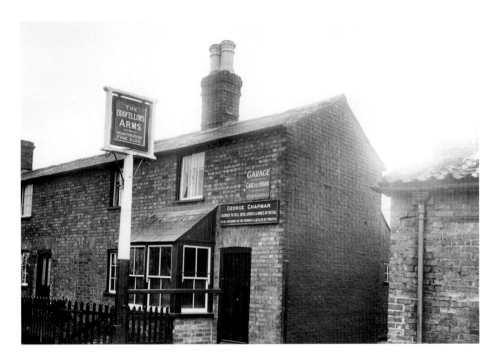

Oddfellows Arms – Church Street, Sawtry

The 'Oddfellows Arms' was at the end of a row of houses. Like many other pubs, it was probably little more than a converted front room. In 1921 it was one of six pubs in Sawtry, at a time when the village had just 909 inhabitants. These days the 6,000 residents have just two pubs. Warren Croft, off Church Street, is named after Frank Warren, one time landlord of the 'Oddfellows Arms'. It was built on the paddock belonging to the pub.

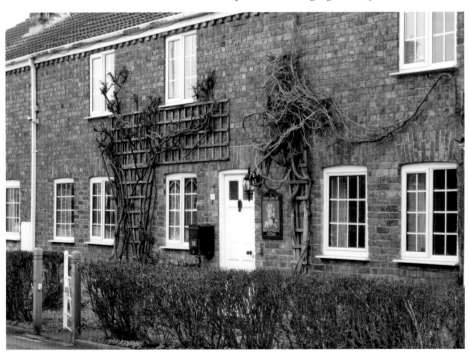

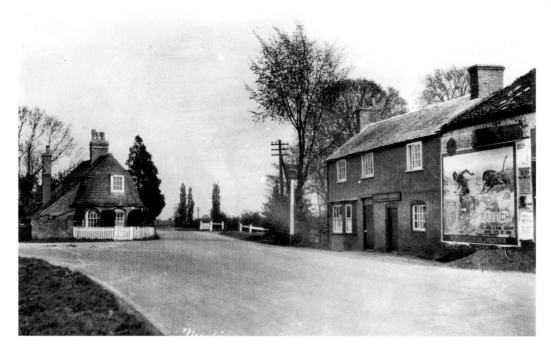

The Manchester Arms – St Audrey's Lane, St Ives

'The Manchester Arms' was named for the Dukes of Manchester, lords of the manor of St Ives. It was a country beerhouse until 1938 when it was licensed for wines and spirits. Business grew as the town expanded. In 1977 it advertised itself as 'a fine old country tavern' with 'tea rooms open in the spring in over 5 acres of grounds'. It is still a pub today.

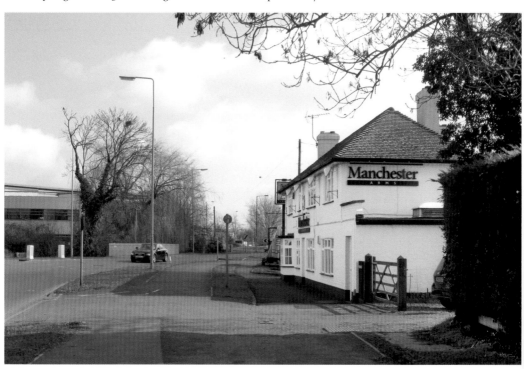

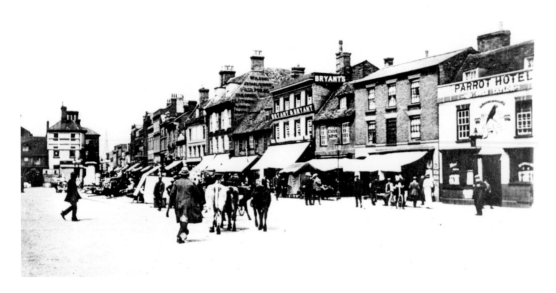

The Parrot – The Pavement, St Ives

This pub became 'The Parrot' in 1800 after having had several names including the 'Macaw'. The pub closed and was demolished in 1932 to make way for the building of a new bank. The building is still a bank today; the site of the former 'Parrot' now forms part of Barclays Bank.

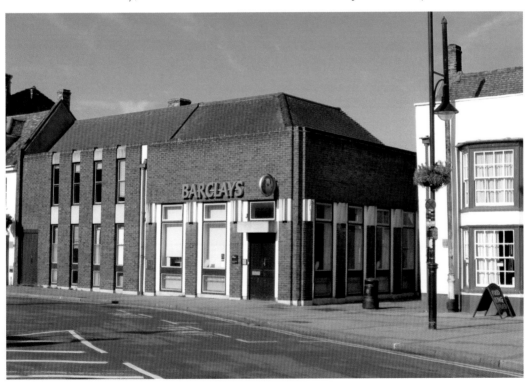

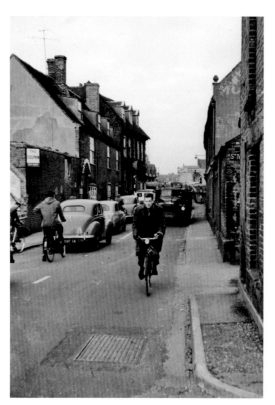

The Dolphin – London Road, St Ives

This pub is first recorded in a parish register entry from 1594. 'The Dolphin' and 'The White Horse' opposite were well placed at the southern end of the medieval bridge. Before the building of the bypass, all traffic from London and the south would have passed this way. Travellers could leave their horses and carriages here and cross the bridge on foot, thereby avoiding the toll. The old 'Dolphin' closed in 1968; the new 'Dolphin' is a completely new building which opened in March 1986 and was further extended during the 1990s.

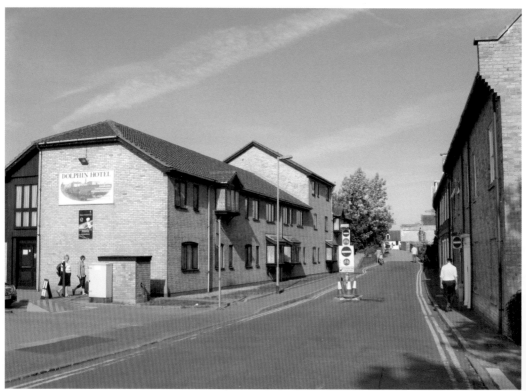

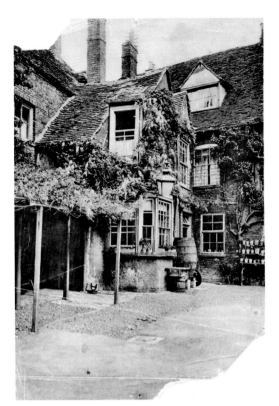

The White Horse – London Road, St Ives
The earliest mention of 'The White Horse' in historical records relates to the murder there of John Hodgson in 1663. The southern part was built around 1700 – both north and south parts of Bridge House formed part of 'The White Horse' until the early nineteenth century. It was taken over by the military in the First World War and never re-opened. It is now Bridge House flats.

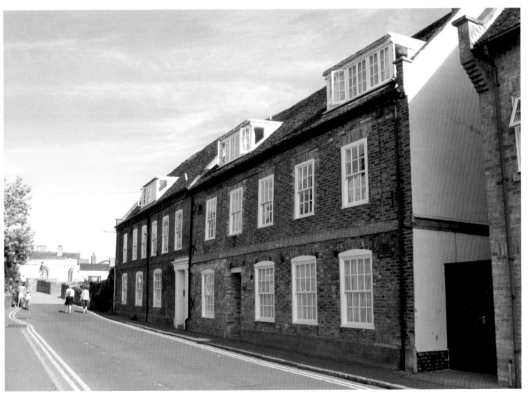

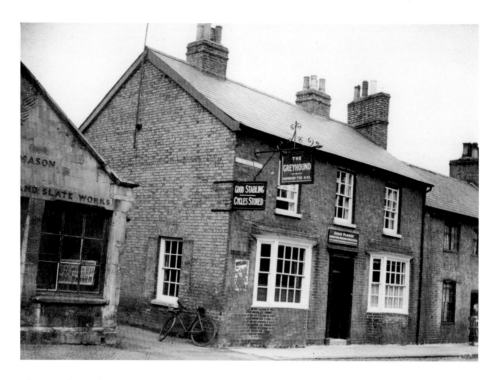

The Greyhound – Carlisle Terrace, St Ives

'The Greyhound' dates from Victorian times and is still trading in Carlisle Terrace. Many of its landlords had other businesses too, including a butcher, a blacksmith, a shoemaker and a chiropodist. One landlord was John Norris, grandfather of Herbert Norris, the St Ives historian for whom the Norris Museum is named.

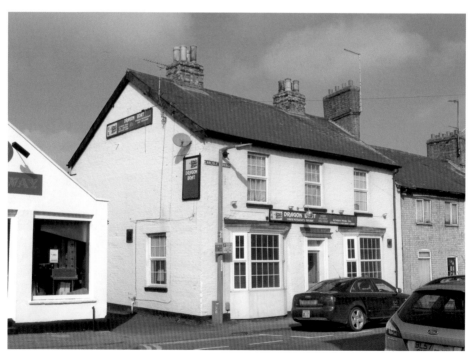

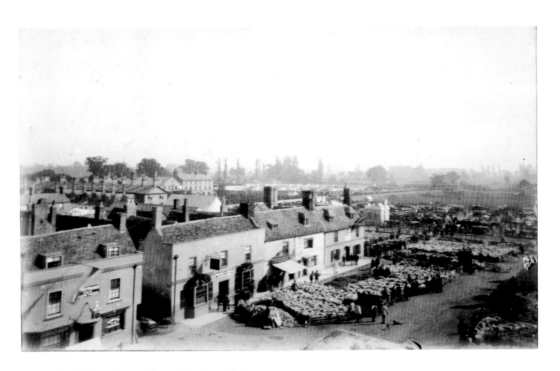

The White Hart – Sheep Market, St Ives

One of the longest established pubs keeping its original name in St Ives; it has been trading for over 300 years. The present building dates from the early eighteenth century. It was probably rebuilt after a fire which started in White Hart Lane in 1689. The old photograph was taken on market day and you can see the sheep in front of the pub. 'The White Hart' is still trading today.

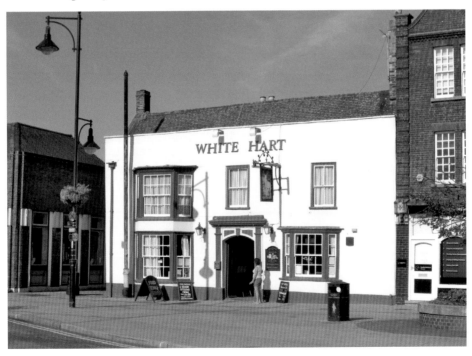

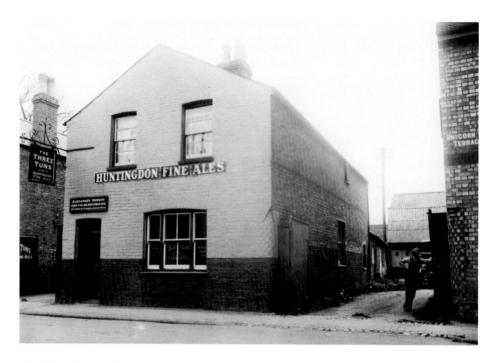

The Three Tuns – West Street, St Ives

'The Three Tuns' in West Street opened in the 1870s after 'The Three Tuns' in Bridge Street closed. When it in turn closed in 1959, the license was transferred by East Anglian Breweries to a new pub, 'The Seven Wives' in Ramsey Road. The building has been demolished although part of the outer wall remains opposite Globe Place car park. You can still make out the 'Unicorn Terrace' sign on the neighbouring house.

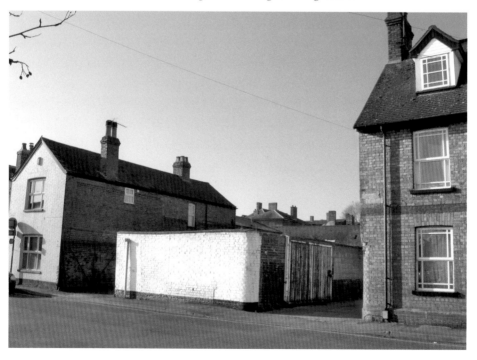

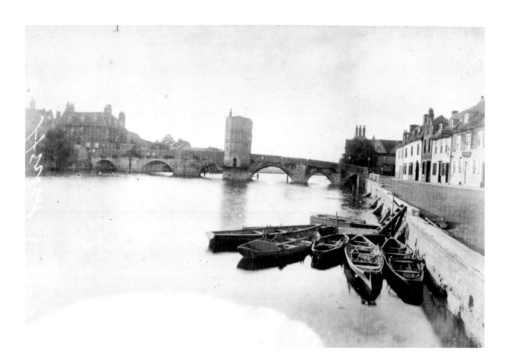

The Ship – The Quay, St Ives

'The Ship' is mentioned in Edmund Pettis' survey in 1720, but it had closed by about 1890. The wines and spirits license was transferred to 'The Oliver Cromwell' which had been only a beerhouse until then. The wrought iron sign bracket also went to 'The Oliver Cromwell'. Most of the building was demolished in 1920. The Number Four restaurant now occupies the site.

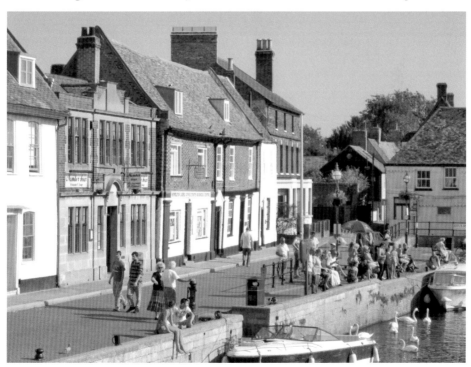

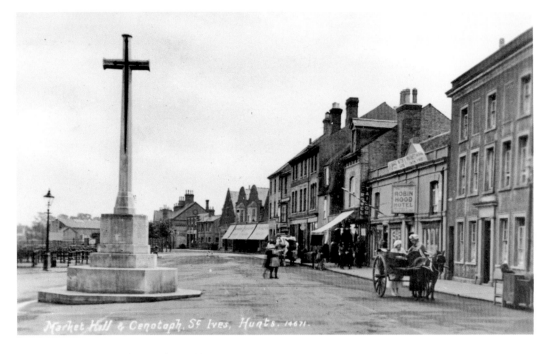

The Robin Hood – Market Hill, St Ives

'The Robin Hood' is still a pub. Originally it was two pubs – 'The Swan' (or 'Three Swans') and 'The Angel'. 'The Swan' had become 'The Robin Hood' (or 'Robin Hood and Little John') by 1795, but 'The Angel' was occupied by several other businesses. It was a hairdresser from the 1850s until 1925. The current pub occupies both buildings which were extensively altered. It was one of the first pubs in St Ives to have a slot machine.

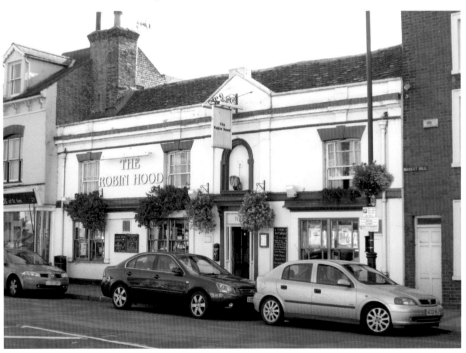

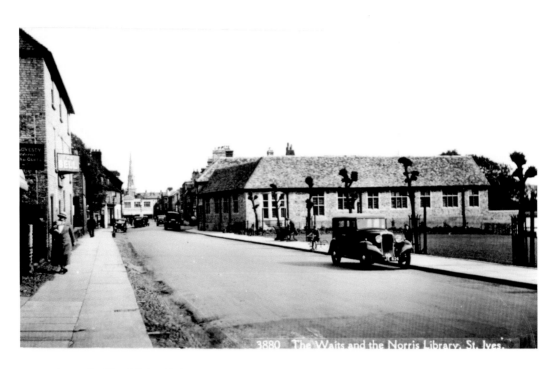

The Bell – The Waits, St Ives

'The Bell' had several changes of name: previously 'The White Swan', then 'The Blue Bell' (1787) then 'The Old Bell', then just 'The Bell'. In Victorian times it became a lodging house for the poorest of travellers, tramps and pedlars. It remained a lodging house until the 1930s and finally closed in 1951. Having a Methodist church next door was not good for business. It is now a private house.

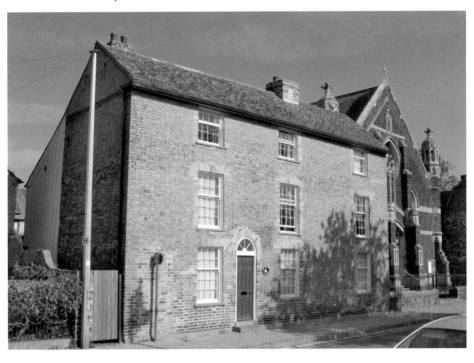

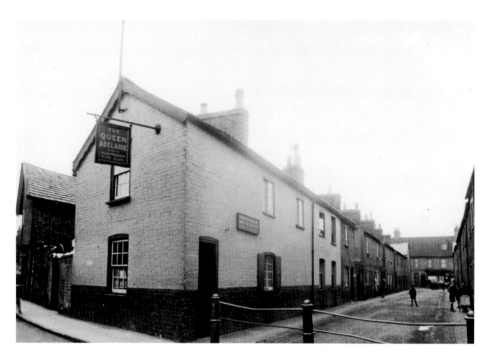

The Queen Adelaide – North Road/Green Street, St Ives

'The Queen Adelaide' began trading in Victorian times and was probably named after the wife of King William IV who died in 1849 during the reign of her niece Queen Victoria. It stood on the corner of Green Street and North Road, which is now part of Globe Place car park. It closed in 1951 and the whole street it stood in was demolished.

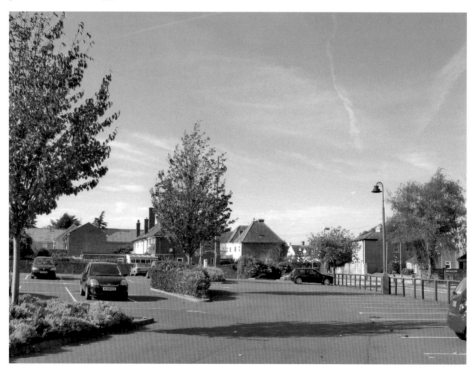

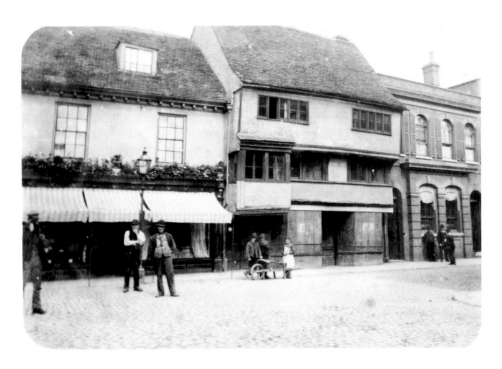

The Salutation Inn – Crown Street, St Ives

'The Salutation' dates from the fifteenth or sixteenth century and was next door to 'The Crown Inn'. The building was used by the Church Temperance Club for a while but was demolished in 1887 to make way for the new post office. This was itself demolished when a new post office was built in Bridge Street. It is now Superdrug.

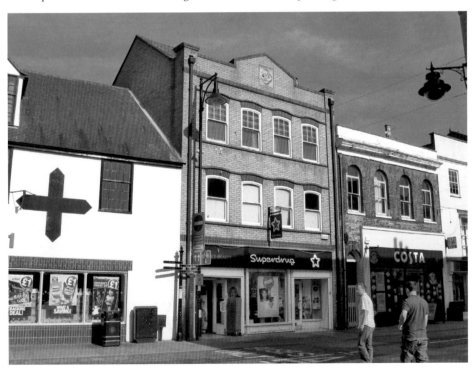

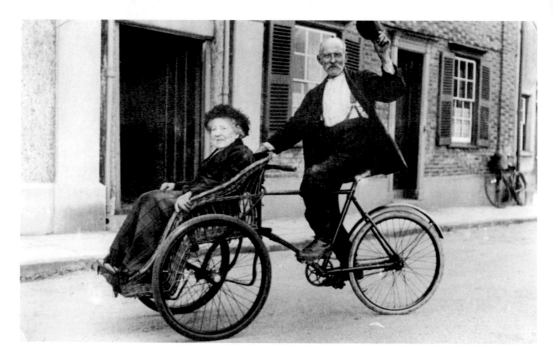

The Chequer – The Quay, St Ives

'The Chequer' was mentioned by the historian Edmund Pettis in 1720. It was also known as 'The Chequer and Anchor'. It was named for the chequer effect of its brickwork. A chequer design on the exterior of a pub usually meant that entertainment was provided inside. The building is now a suite of offices.

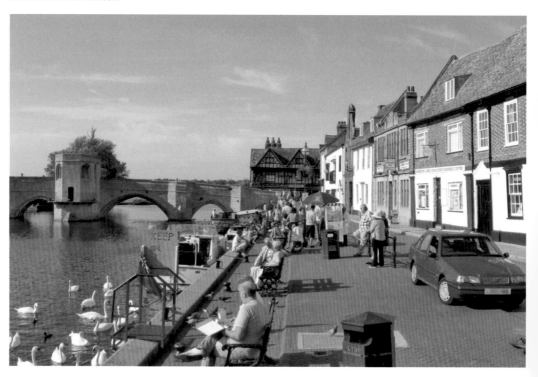

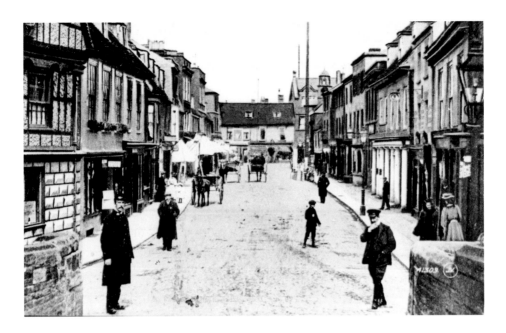

The Crown – Crown Street, St Ives

'The Crown' is first recorded in 1684, but is probably older. In coaching days this was the biggest and most important inn around St Ives. In the 1720s, it was worth more than double any other property in the town. The coming of the railway led to its decline and parts of the building were let out as shops. It closed completely in the 1930s. The building survived until 1975 when it was destroyed by fire. The modern building is a copy of the original. For many years it was Woolworth's, but is now Poundland.

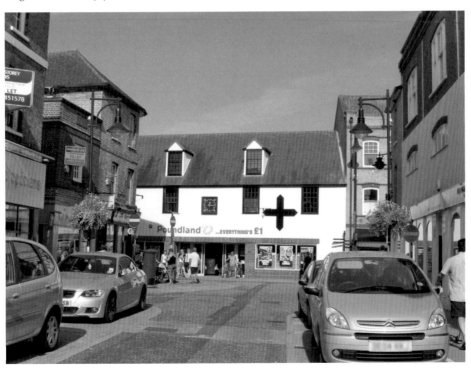

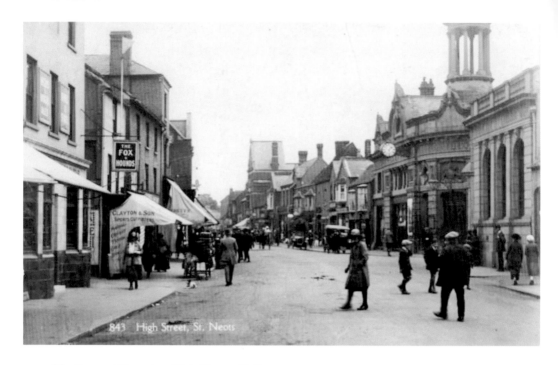

843 High Street, St. Neots

The Fox and Hounds – High Street, St Neots

'The Fox and Hounds' was probably built around 1700. It had cottages and a small brew house in the yard. There was also a small Baptist chapel there, whose members were known locally as the 'tally-ho baptists'. The pub closed in 1962 and was refurbished into an off-license selling beer, wines and spirits for Peatling & Cawdron Ltd. The premises are now the offices of an estate agent.

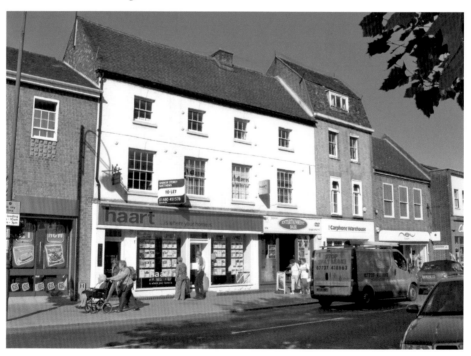

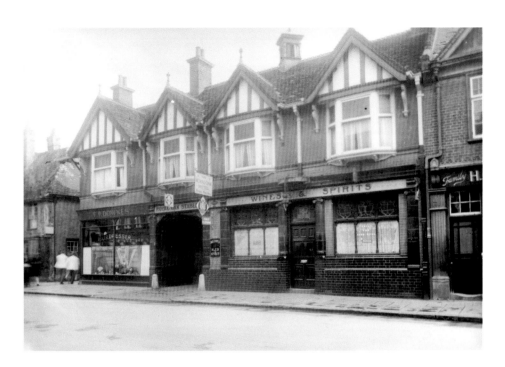

The Royal Oak – High Street, St Neots

The present building was built in 1885 to replace a much smaller inn. Before rebuilding it had a shop window on the west side which was used as a wine shop and off-licence. In 'The Royal Oak yard' there were six cottages, butchers' stables and a slaughterhouse. It was often called 'Chessum's yard' after the family who ran the slaughterhouse. The building is not much changed, but is now occupied by the Halifax bank.

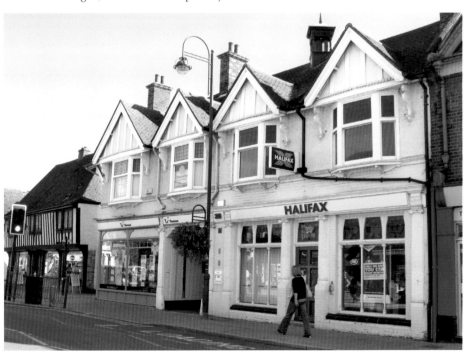

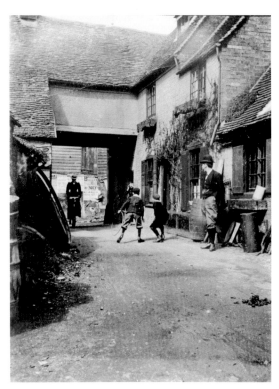

The King's Head – South Street, St Neots

'The Kings Head' is still in business, although it has been much altered since the old photograph was taken around 100 years ago. The photographs show the yard; the clutter of barrels and pile of horse droppings in the old photograph are typical of an old inn yard. They have been replaced by the trappings of a modern pub yard.

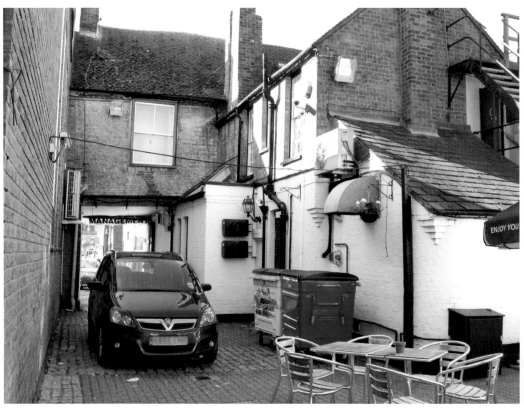

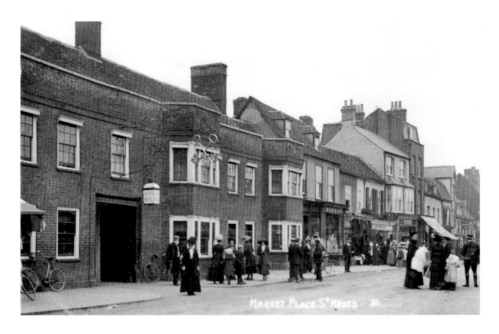

The Cross Keys – Market Square, St Neots

'The Cross Keys' dates from the seventeenth century. It was probably here that the Earl of Holland was staying in July 1648 when the Parliamentary Army attacked St Neots. Following the battle the Royalist Earl was captured. Before the coming of the railway it was a coaching inn with coaches to London, Glasgow, Oxford and Cambridge leaving from here. When the railway opened, a horse omnibus met every train. It closed in the 1980s but the façade survives as a shopping mall.

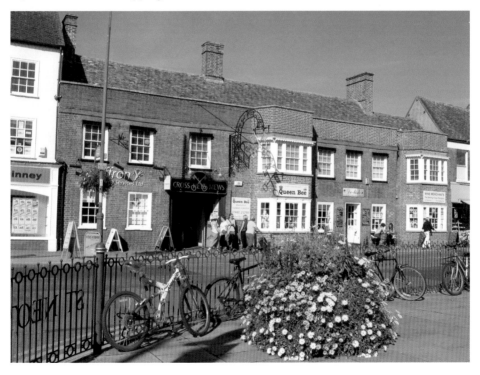

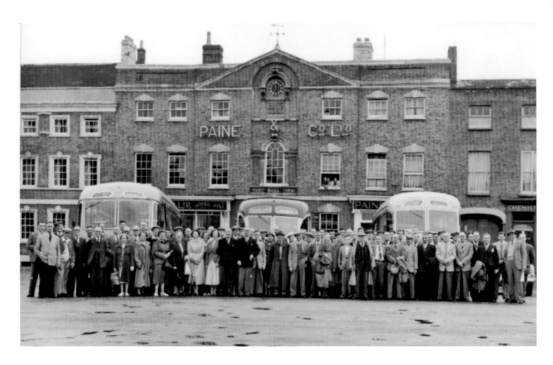

Paine's Brewery – Market Square, St Neots

The history of the brewery can be traced back to the 1700s. James Paine, a farmer who owned Toseland Manor, bought the brewery in 1831. At its peak the brewery controlled twenty-five retail outlets from Sawtry to Sandy. The old photograph shows workers preparing to leave on an outing. In 1982, the brewery business was sold and the building stood empty until 1998 when it was converted to offices and shops. The frontage on the market square has been preserved.

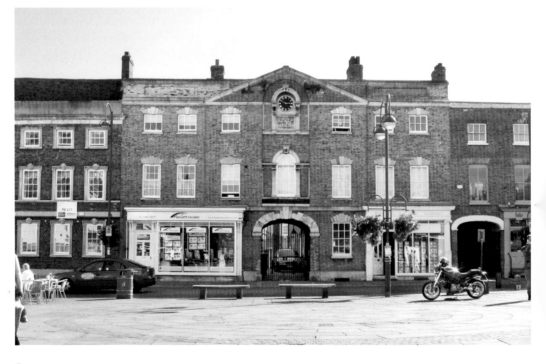

The (White) Swan – Brook Street, St Neots

'The Swan' or 'White Swan' is now a row of cottages. Until 1913, it was a waterside inn frequented by the bargemen and carters working at the Brookside wharf. The earliest known landlord is John Squire (1708–60). The inn had its license withdrawn in 1913. For several years after, a painted sign offering 'Pony and trap for Hire' could be seen on the front of the building.

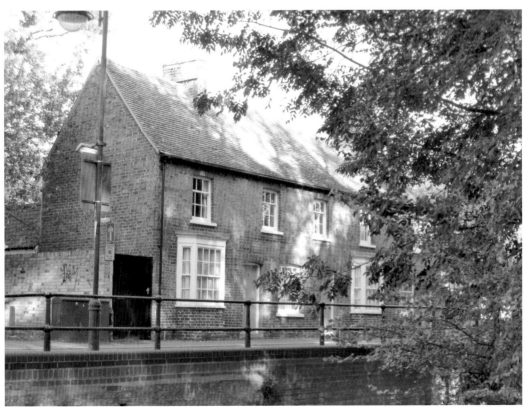

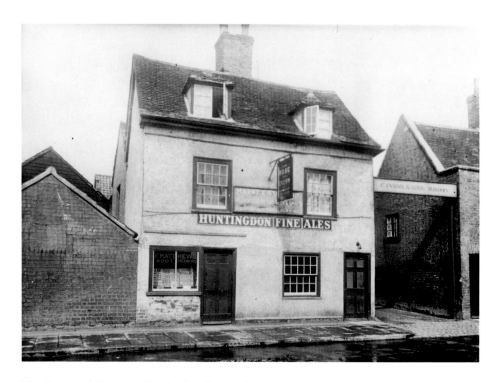

The Rose and Crown – Cambridge Street, St Neots

'The Rose and Crown' had been a pub since 1809, one of several at the town end of Cambridge Street. 'The Jolly Brewers' (later 'The Two Brewers') was next door and 'The Plough Inn' a little further along (this became a builder's yard and is now the Spar shop). 'The Rose and Crown' continued trading until the 1980s and is now a private house. The buildings on either side have been demolished.

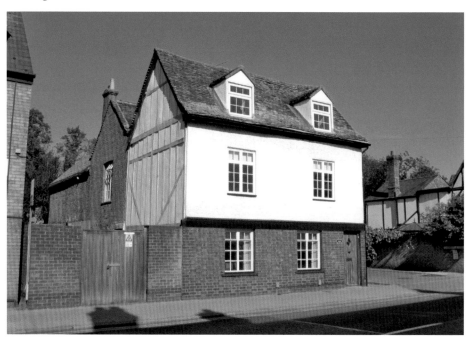

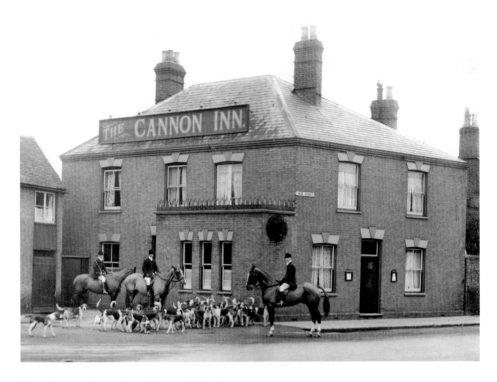

The Cannon Inn – New Street, St Neots

'The Cannon Inn' stood on the corner of New Street and Bedford Street, which in 1878 was known as Hyde Park Corner. There was an inn there in 1809 and until 1859 it was known as 'The Old Cannon'. It was rebuilt in the nineteenth century with extensive stabling to accommodate the horses and vehicles of farmers coming to the market and New Street sale yards. It is still a pub, these days called 'The Hyde Park'.

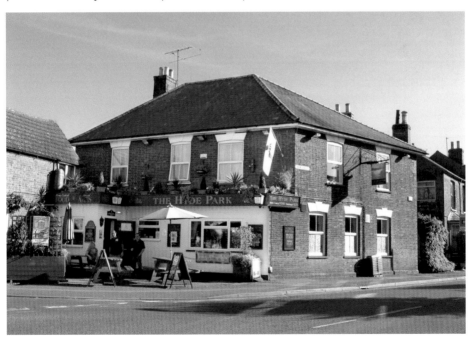

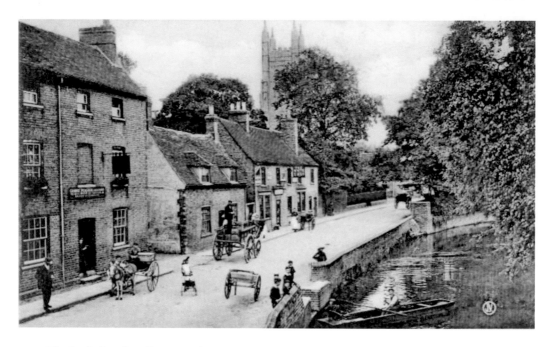

The Bushel and Strike – Brook Street, St Neots

The building is unusual in having two upper floors. For many years 'The Bushel and Strike' was an inn and common lodging house where, according to Tebbutt, 'tramps, Italian organ-grinders and other pedestrian travellers could hire a bed for as little as 2*d* a night'. It had a bad reputation and the police were often summoned to break up drunken brawls and knife fights. These days there is an altogether more peaceful scene along Brook Street.

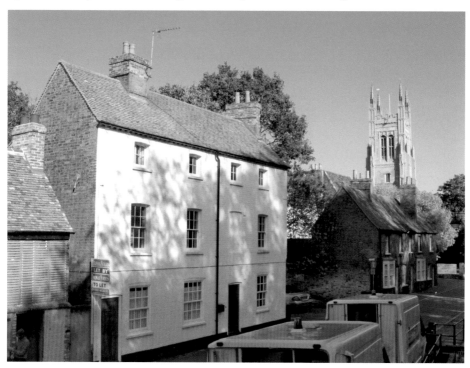

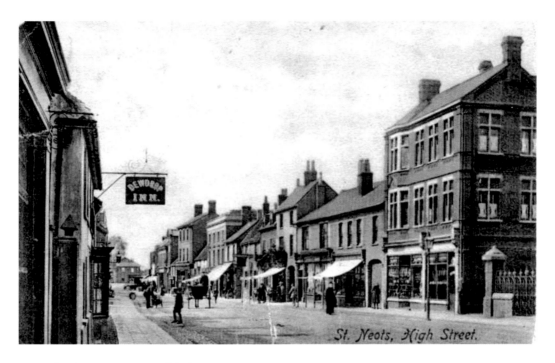

The Dew Drop Inn – High Street, St Neots

'The Dew Drop Inn' dated from the seventeenth century and, like many businesses along the High Street, it had a cottage in the yard at the back. The name may be a pun on 'do drop in'. The inn has been replaced by a row of shops built in 1984, currently occupied by a takeaway.

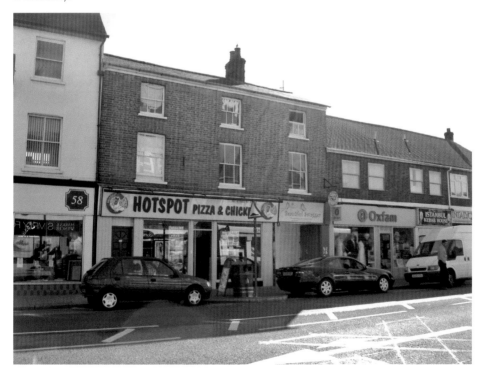

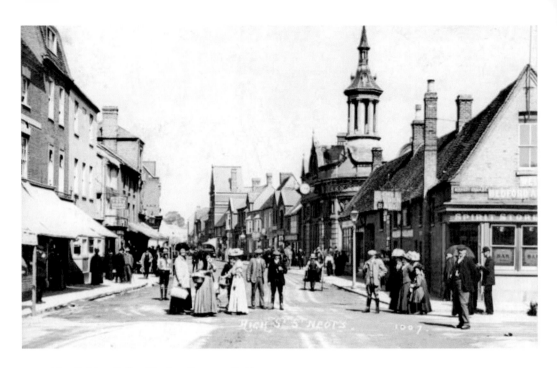

The Golden Ball – Market Square, St Neots

'The Golden Ball' was rebuilt in 1935; before that it had been a timber-framed house. It may at some time have formed part of the Court Hall, a sixteenth-century hall which dominated the market square, where the lord of the manor would administer the town's affairs. 'The Golden Ball' became prosperous during the days of the Vulcan Iron works as it was a meeting place for the men working there. It has now been renamed 'The Corner House'.

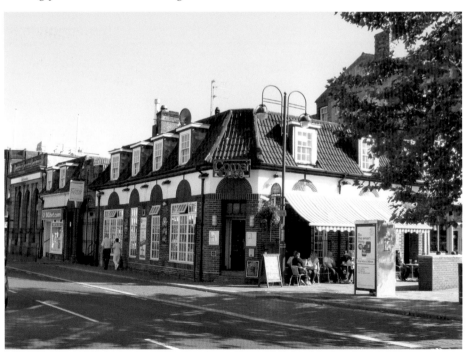

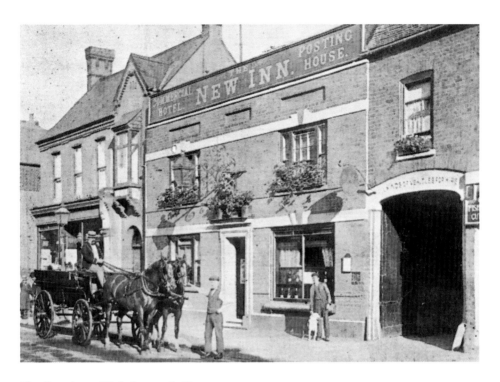

The New Inn – High Street, St Neots

'The New Inn' was once a posting house where coaches would stop to change their horses. It had extensive yards at the back that included stabling and a malting. Next to the inn was 'The New Inn Tap' which in the nineteenth century served working men who were not welcome at the hotel. In 1911 this became a hairdresser's shop. The pub itself is still trading and was fully refurbished in 2010.

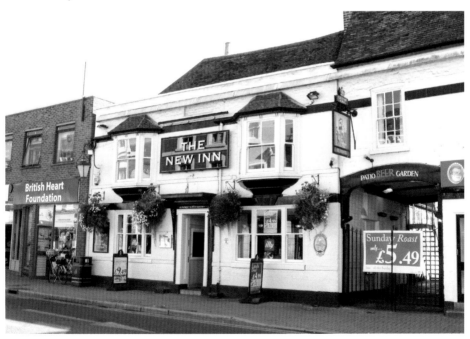

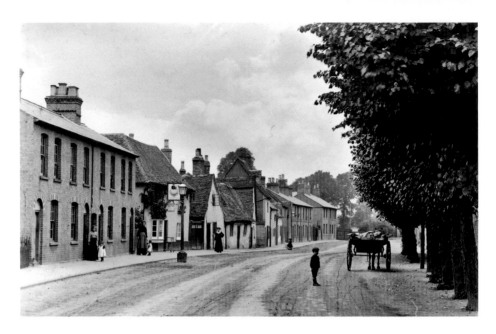

The Globe – Huntingdon Street, St Neots

'The Globe' was in a run-down area frequented by workers from the paper mill. Its most distinguishing feature was the pictorial sign – a globe from which protruded the head and shoulders of 'the struggler'. On the reverse were the lines:

> *Assist the struggler*
> *My friend and brother*
> *And through this world*
> *We'll help each other.*

At the time the modern photograph was taken, the building was for sale.

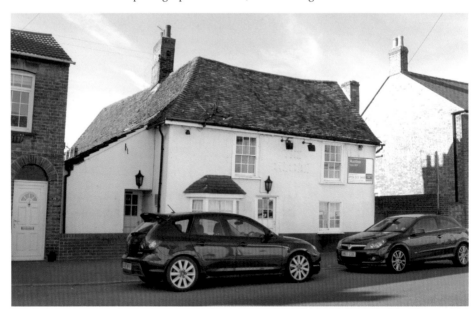

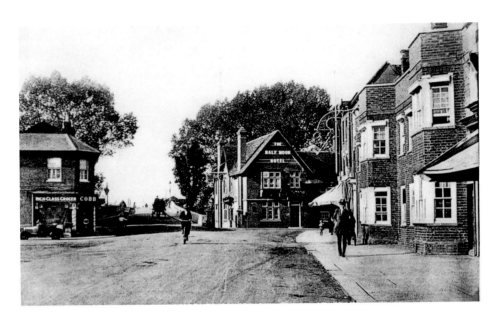

The Half Moon – Market Square, St Neots

'The Half Moon' dates back to at least the sixteenth century. Part of the frontage was once a butcher's shop. The success of Charles Gill's houseboats on the river in attracting visitors to the area and popularising the town as a holiday destination gave the trade at 'The Half Moon' a huge boost. The name changed to 'The Bridge' in 1912 when it was rebuilt as a hotel. It is still trading and now known as 'Bridge House'.

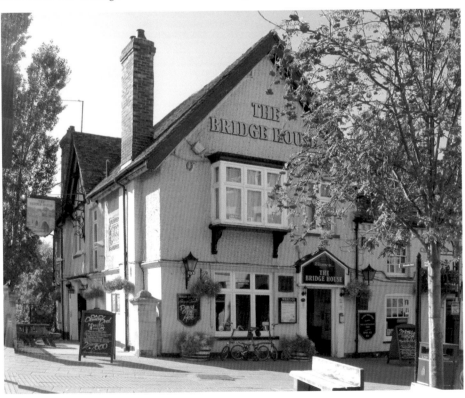

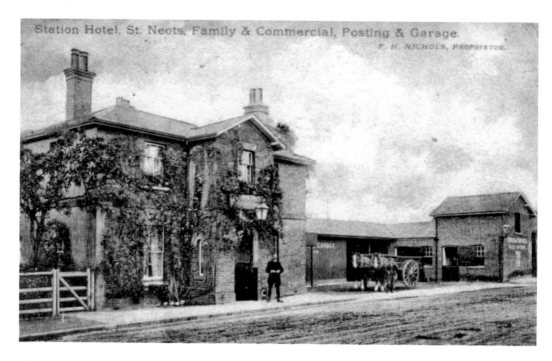

Station Hotel, St. Neots, Family & Commercial, Posting & Garage.

F. H. NICHOLS, PROPRIETOR.

The Station Hotel – St Neots

'The Station Hotel' (or 'Railway Inn') is first mentioned in 1858. The railway station had opened a few years earlier with the building of the Great Northern Line in 1850. It offered an 'excellent waiting room, serving refreshments at the lowest prices.' As is the case with many railway hotels, it was demolished and is now the site of a small car park near this industrial estate.

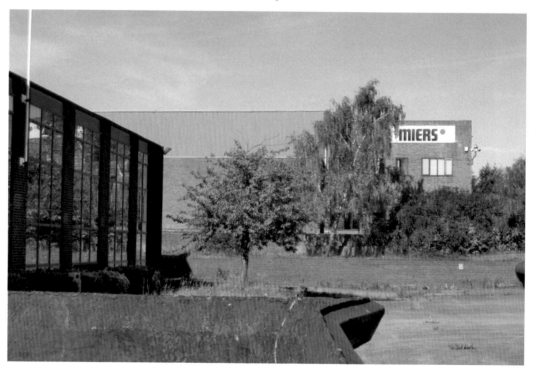

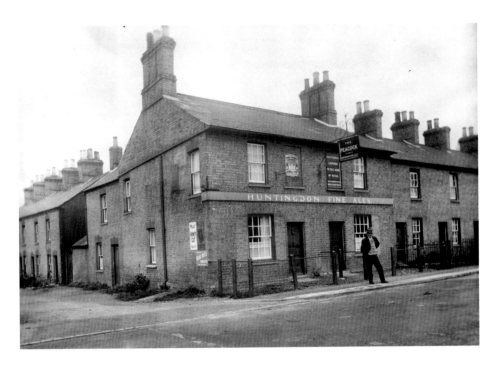

The Peacock – Cambridge Street, St Neots

'The Peacock' beerhouse was first recorded in 1855. It stood at the end of a row of houses in Cambridge Street. 'The Engine and Tender' was next door. The two pubs probably benefitted from being between the town centre and the railway station. The buildings next door have now been demolished and the building stands semi-derelict between a Spar store and an office supplier.

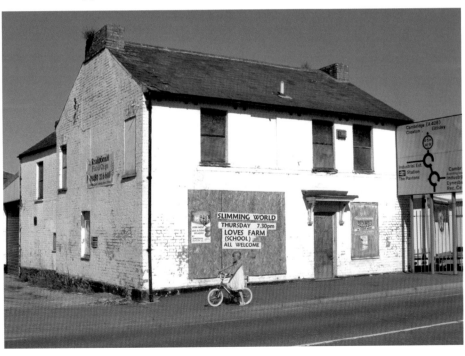

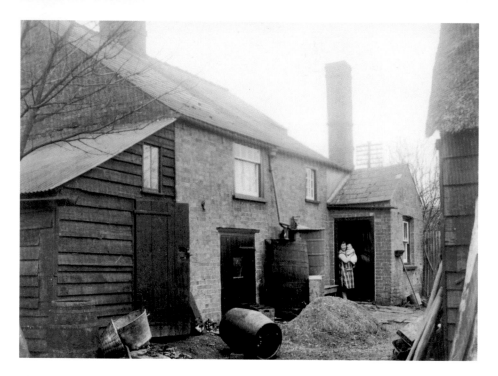

The Royal Oak – Upwood

The name 'Royal Oak' alludes to the escape of Prince Charles after the Battle of Worcester in 1651. Charles is alleged to have evaded capture by hiding in an oak tree near Boscobel House, Staffordshire. Charles later became King Charles II when the monarchy was restored in 1660. The name became popular for pubs across the country. This 'Royal Oak' was a beerhouse in Little London. It closed in 1952 and is now a private house on the corner of Royal Oak Close.

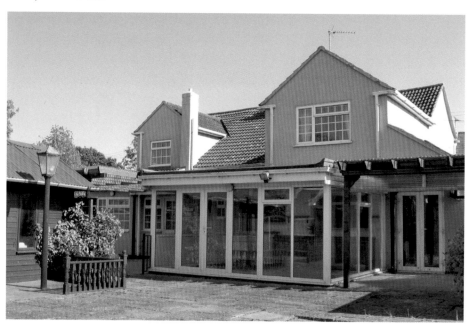

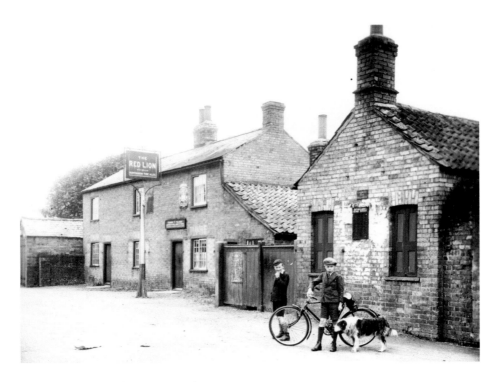

The Red Lion – High Street, Warboys

'The Red Lion' or 'Lyon' as it appears in the 1891 census was a beerhouse. At that time it was being run by seventy-one year old widow Rachel Henson who had taken over the business from her husband William. There are twenty beer retailers listed in the Warboys directory of 1903, in addition to several public houses – they could not all remain in business and the former 'Red Lion' is now a private house.

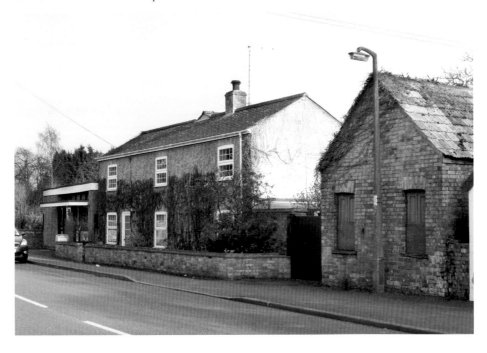

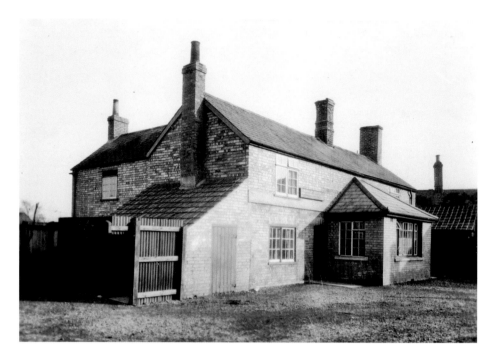

The Royal Oak – Station Road, Warboys

'The Royal Oak' began life as an alehouse for workers at the nearby mill. The pub belonged to the Fellowes family which acquired the Ramsey Abbey estate in 1737. In 1801 'The Royal Oak' became a public house. The old photograph was taken in 1930 when the licensee was Harold Clack. The corrugated fence at the side of the building is the shared ladies and gents toilet of the time. 'The Royal Oak' is still a pub, but the toilets are now inside the building!

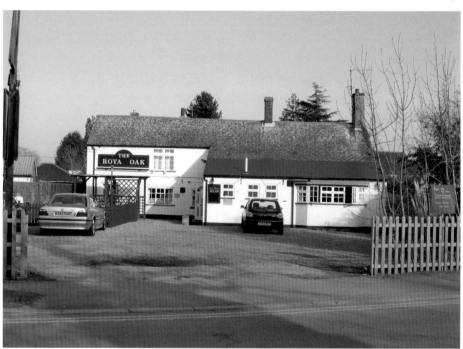

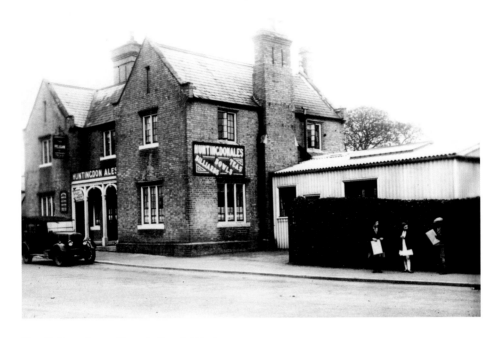

The Pelican Inn – Church Road, Warboys

'The Pelican Inn' was probably named after the ship on which Sir Francis Drake was knighted by Queen Elizabeth I; its former owner had a financial stake in the ship. The present building was constructed around 1800. After ownership by several different breweries, the buildings fell into disrepair and the 'Pelican' closed in 1972. In 1973, it was sold and houses were built on either side of the main building. The former pub was purchased and restored to its former glory in 2003.

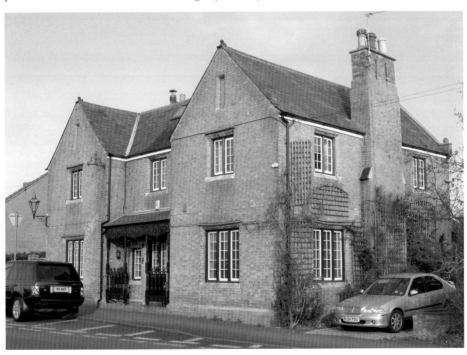

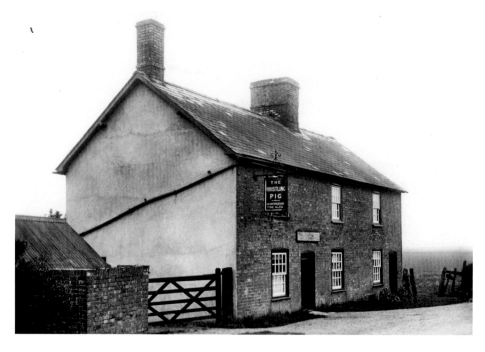

The Whistling Pig – Heath Drove, Warboys

'The Whistling Pig', 'The Golden Drop' and 'The Carpenters Arms' were all beerhouses on Heath Drove, which is now the main road to Chatteris. The 1891 census records 127 agricultural labourers living in this area – farming was thirsty work. 'The Whistling Pig' was run by Benjamin Whitsey who was also an agricultural labourer. It remained in the family for many years with Jane Whitsey and then Mary Ann Whitsey taking over. It is now the Africandawns dog training centre and boarding kennels.

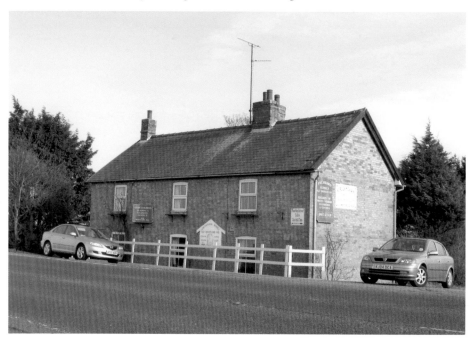